COUNTRY DIAGNOSTIC STUDY ON LONG-TERM CARE IN SRI LANKA

JULY 2021

ASIAN DEVELOPMENT BANK

ADB

Notes: In this publication, "$" refers to United States dollars, and "SLR" refers to Sri Lankan rupee.
ADB recognizes "China" as the People's Republic of China.

On the cover: As Sri Lanka's population ages, the need for care among older persons also increases, presenting social
and economic challenges to families, policymakers and other stakeholders (photos from ADB Photo Library).

Printed on recycled paper

CONTENTS

TABLES, FIGURES, AND BOXES

FOREWORD

Rapid aging in Asia and the Pacific has put the region at the forefront of one of the most important global trends. The demographic shift is largely the result of both increased longevity and decreased fertility rates, which are both examples of development success. The change is happening at an unprecedented pace: in 2020, 13% of the population in the Asia and Pacific region is aged 60 or above, and by 2050, it is expected to increase to 24%, or roughly 1.3 billion people. At the same time, traditional family support systems are weakening due to increased migration, urbanization, decreasing family sizes, and expanding female labor market participation. Even when family care support is available, people with complex care needs and their caregivers require additional support.

The demographic, economic, and social trends are resulting in a growing need to establish and finance long-term care (LTC) services and develop the enabling environments to support older people to age well and help families and communities to care for their older citizens. The development of models of care that are affordable, sustainable, accessible, efficacious, and adapted to local contexts is sorely needed.

The window of opportunity to plan for, prepare, and adapt to the needs of aging populations is now. There is great diversity among countries in the region. Some are aging at a fast rate and need to adapt quickly, others will age slower, but will end up with very large older populations. What is common, however, is that countries in the region will see change in the coming years and need to prepare for it. The coronavirus disease (COVID-19) pandemic and its disproportionate impacts on older persons and on existing care systems have illustrated how important it is to strengthen existing systems and develop new capacities.

The Asian Development Bank (ADB) has a growing portfolio on LTC, and is working to capitalize on opportunities of increased population longevity and help mitigate the social and fiscal risks of population aging. In May 2016, ADB approved the regional capacity development technical assistance for the Strengthening Developing Member Countries' Capacity in Elderly Care project, to help increase the capacity of developing member countries to design policies and plans for the improvement of their LTC services. The six diverse countries included in this regional technical assistance are Indonesia, Mongolia, Sri Lanka, Thailand, Tonga, and Viet Nam.

The technical assistance aims to (i) build a knowledge base in the region for the development of LTC systems and services; (ii) improve the capacity of officials and other stakeholders in these countries to design and implement strategic LTC plans; and (iii) create a network for disseminating knowledge, good practices, and expertise.

This country diagnostic study aims to help strengthen the knowledge base on emerging LTC policies, programs, and systems in Sri Lanka. The study outlines findings on the current situation of LTC with regard to the need for care and the supply of care, regulatory and policy frameworks, service provision, quality management, human resources, and financing. Analysis, conclusions, and recommendations concerning LTC system development are also included and have been informed by an in-country consultative process.

Population aging is a key megatrend of the 21st century, and how the Asia and Pacific region adapts to this trend will be an important factor in the continued development of the region. ADB is committed to working with our members on this journey.

Bruno Carrasco
Director General concurrently Chief Compliance Officer
Sustainable Development and Climate Change Department
Asian Development Bank

ACKNOWLEDGMENTS

This publication was prepared under the regional technical assistance for Strengthening Developing Member Countries' Capacity in Elderly Care project (TA 9111) by the Social Development Thematic Group of the Asian Development Bank (ADB). The report is one of six country diagnostic assessments—done for Indonesia, Mongolia, Sri Lanka, Thailand, Tonga, and Viet Nam—that examine existing elderly care policies, services, and systems, including identification of gaps and opportunities toward long-term care development. Wendy Walker, chief of the Social Development Thematic Group, Sustainable Development and Climate Change Department, provided overall guidance and technical advice to the study, with support from Yukiko Ito, Imelda Marquez, Rizza Loise Aguilar-Crisanto, and Maria Genieve Edar. ADB colleagues from the South Asia Human and Social Development Division provided strong support by sharing insights and feedback throughout the implementation of TA 9111 in-country activities in Sri Lanka, including Sungsup Ra, director; Sunhwa Lee, principal social sector specialist; Gi Soon Song, principal social sector specialist; Uzma Hoque, principal social sector specialist; Brian Chin, senior health specialist (now with Central and West Asia Social Sector Division); Jayati Nigam, health specialist (now with East Asia Urban and Social Sectors Division); and Unika Shrestha, young professional. Sri Lanka Resident Mission's Utzav Kumar, senior country economist; and Herathbanda Jayasundara, social development officer, extended huge help in coordinating with the various government agencies and offices.

The Sri Lanka country diagnostic study has been a collective effort, and ADB extends its gratitude to all those who participated as key informants in the study and facilitated the group consultations and focus group discussions, especially the 12 elders from Padakka town of Colombo for their invaluable time, insights, and experiences. ADB thanks the TA 9111 consultants who contributed to the completion of the diagnostic report, namely (i) K.C.S Dalpadatu, R. P. Rannan-Eliya, and their team from Sri Lanka's Institute for Health Policy for producing the final draft report; and (ii) Meredith Wyse and HelpAge International, Usa Khiewrord, Caitlin Littleton, Peter Morrison, Wendy Holmes, Tassannee Surawana, and Rachanichol Arunoprayote for administering and guiding the Sri Lanka diagnostic study team.

ADB expresses its huge appreciation to the members of the Sri Lanka Diagnostic Study Working Group for supporting the study led by S.S. Singappuli, former director, National Secretariat for Elders; M.K. Bandula Harischandra, additional secretary (Social Development), then Ministry of Social Empowerment and Welfare; Ananda Jayalal, former director, and Shiromi Maduwage, acting director, Youth, Elderly, Disabled and Displaced, Ministry of Health (MOH); Harischandra Yakandawala, chairperson, Village 60+; Samantha Liyanawaduge, executive director, HelpAge Sri Lanka; Achala Balasuriya, secretary of the Board of Studies in Geriatric Medicine, Postgraduate Institute of Medicine; and P. Ananthan, deputy director, Non-Communicable Disease Unit, MOH.

The financial support from the Japan Fund for Poverty Reduction and the Republic of Korea e-Asia Knowledge Partnership Fund, both administered by ADB, is acknowledged with gratitude.

ABBREVIATIONS

ADB	Asian Development Bank
ADL	activities of daily living
CDS	country diagnostic study
DMC	developing member country
ERPO	Elder Rights Promotion Officer
IADL	instrumental activities of daily living
IHP	Institute for Health Policy
KII	key informant interview
LTC	long-term care
MOH	Ministry of Health
NCE	National Council for Elders
NGO	nongovernment organization
NSE	National Secretariat for Elders
NVQ	National Vocational Qualification
OECD	Organisation for Economic Co-operation and Development
PDHS	Provincial Director of Health Services
PGIM	Postgraduate Institute of Medicine
PHSRC	Private Health Sector Regulatory Council
SLAGM	Sri Lanka Association of Geriatric Medicine
WHO	World Health Organization
YED MOH	Directorate for Youth, Elderly and Disabled Persons, Ministry of Health

EXECUTIVE SUMMARY

Sri Lanka's population is aging rapidly due to rising life expectancy. Projections show that more than 25% of the population will be over 60 years of age by 2050. As the population ages, the need for care among older persons in Sri Lanka also increases, presenting social and economic challenges that older individuals and families will have to face and that policymakers and other stakeholders will have to prepare for.

This country diagnostic study analyzes Sri Lanka's shifting demographics and presents results of its survey on the current state of eldercare services in the country. The study considers the growing need to provide long-term care (LTC) and other services, and examines educational, institutional, and policy changes that may be undertaken to meet this need.

The study includes a gender and poverty analysis and identifies opportunities for learning, dialogue, and action. The study examines financing options and concludes by presenting recommendations for a national strategy for a system for LTC for older persons.

Key Findings

- Sri Lanka is a lower-middle-income country facing a rapidly aging population resulting from an accelerating decline in fertility and an increase in life expectancy since the 1950s.
- In 2000, 8% of the population was over 60 years of age, growing to 12% in 2012. More than 25% of the population will be over 60 years of age by 2050.
- The need for LTC among older persons is rising. At the same time, traditional family support systems are weakening due to shrinking households, increased migration, and expanding female participation in the labor market.
- Eldercare is provided primarily by family members and domestic helpers in the home. State-funded and private centers and clubs provide a variety of daytime and residential services that allow elders to socialize and remain active.
- Formal LTC services are inadequate to meet current and future needs.

Key Recommendations

- Sri Lanka needs to formulate a nationwide LTC strategy to respond to the rising need to provide care for the country's aging population.
- Legal, policy, and strategy frameworks for LTC must be formulated through government leadership to ensure financing, planning, and quality management of an overall LTC system.
- Various sectors (e.g., health, social protection, urban development, transport) and stakeholders will need to be involved in developing strategies, plans, and policies. Public awareness and engagement will also be crucial to the success of an LTC system.

- Home- and community-based services should be the primary approach. Residential care should also be available.
- There is a need to build a workforce for LTC services. Training for formal and informal caregivers, health professionals, and social welfare staff should be developed to increase the number and improve the quality of the LTC workforce.
- Sustainable financing must be ensured for LTC. Developing a public financing model for LTC is essential to expand LTC services throughout the country.

I. BACKGROUND AND COUNTRY CONTEXT

Sri Lanka faces a transition to a rapidly aging population. The total population was 20.3 million at the last national census in 2012. In 2000, 9.2% of the population was older than 60 years of age compared to 11% in 2006, 12% in 2015, and 15.9% in 2019.[1] This proportion of older persons is only marginally smaller than the same projection for member countries of the Organisation for Economic Co-operation and Development (OECD). Furthermore, the total population is expected to decline after 2030, thus increasing old-age dependency ratios. Box 1 provides some statistics on Sri Lanka.

The rapid aging of the population is attributed to two key factors: declining fertility since the 1950s, and increasing life expectancy. The total fertility rate was estimated at 5.32 children per woman in 1953, 3.45 in 1981, and 2.25 in 2011.[2] Although earlier projections suggested that this rate would fall close to 1.5 by 2020,[3] recent data indicate that the fertility rate will remain above replacement level at least until 2022, due to higher than anticipated fertility among women aged 35–49 years and teenagers.[4] Life expectancy in 2012 was 74.9 years. On average, Sri Lankans currently live longer. Life expectancy is expected to reach levels on a par with OECD member countries, and is projected to reach 77.8 years by 2050.[5]

The Government of Sri Lanka has a long history of funding health care and other basic constitutional freedoms (e.g., education and social services) for its citizens. This has helped increase life expectancy and reduce the total fertility rate. In the past few decades, Sri Lanka's economy and society have undergone major structural changes that present substantial challenges in providing social protection. By establishing major social protection schemes for education, health, and nutrition, and their impacts, the government has cemented public expectation that it will intervene to address and fund key social disparities. This belief is an integral part of the social contract and a basis for social stability.

Older Sri Lankans have lived through several key events that have implications on their well-being in later life, including the attainment of independence in 1948 and overall growth in the economy and development, partly due to economic liberalization and progressive policies adopted since 1977. These events also include a long period of civil conflict between ethnic groups, which particularly affected some older Sri Lankans (e.g., those who fought in the conflict, lost children, or were displaced). Natural disasters—particularly floods, droughts, storms, and sea surges—are common. The 2004 Indian Ocean Tsunami claimed 35,000 lives and displaced over 500,000 people.

---

[1] Calculation based on United Nations. 2019. *World Population Prospects: The 2019 Revision*. New York.

[2] T. De Silva. 2008. *Low Fertility Trends: Causes, Consequences and Policy Options*. Colombo, Sri Lanka: Institute for Health Policy; and A.T.P.L. Abeykoon, R. Rannan-Eliya, and R. Wickremasinghe. 2013. *Study on Maternity Protection Insurance in Sri Lanka*. Colombo: Institute for Health Policy.

[3] World Bank. 2008. *Sri Lanka: Addressing the Needs of an Aging Population*. Human Development Unit, South Asia Region.

[4] L. Dissanayake. 2017. Making the Connection: Population Dynamics and Development in Sri Lanka. *UNFPA Population Matters Policy*. Issue 03.

[5] World Health Organization. 2015. *World Report on Ageing and Health*. Geneva.

Location contributes to the diversity of elders' experiences. In the 2012 census, about 77% of Sri Lankans lived in rural areas compared to 18% in urban areas and 4% on estates (plantations).[6] In the hill country, isolation, cooler temperatures, and steep pathways may present particular difficulties for elders who need support care. Coastal communities with tourism, fishing villages, urban Colombo, and post-conflict areas all have unique environments, systems, and needs.

Because Sri Lanka lacks a national definition of LTC, stakeholders may be unfamiliar with or have differing understandings of key terminology. In its 2015 *World Report on Ageing and Health*, the World Health Organization (WHO) defined LTC as "activities undertaken by others to ensure that people with or at risk of a significant ongoing loss of intrinsic capacity can maintain a level of functional ability consistent with their basic rights, fundamental freedoms and human dignity." The present study defined LTC for older persons as "medical, nursing, personal and social care services provided over a sustained period of time to assist persons who are unable to perform activities of daily living (ADL) and instrumental activities of daily living (IADL) and ensure that they are able to live the remainder of their lives in comfort consistent with their basic human rights and freedoms." While the broader WHO definition leads to a more holistic, person-centered approach to care and care practices, the second definition articulates more clearly the key elements of LTC to key stakeholders. In the context of LTC in Sri Lanka, "older persons" refer to those aged 60+ years.

The Government of Sri Lanka has provided its citizens with health, education, and social welfare services for many decades, funded through general tax revenue. The government plays a prominent role in regulating, funding, and providing health, education, and social services. These are formal systems because they are regulated, established, funded, and operated by the government. Therefore, "formal LTC system" in this report refers to a system to provide LTC services that is regulated, financed, and monitored by the government. Establishing a sustainable and formal LTC system in Sri Lanka will require government financing and involvement. Notably, the currently very limited LTC services available to elders cannot be considered a formal LTC system.

---

6   Government of Sri Lanka, Department of Census and Statistics. 2012. *Census of Population and Housing: Sri Lanka.* http://www.statistics.gov.lk/PopHouSat/CPH2011/Pages/Activities/Reports/SriLanka.pdf.

Box 1: Country Context—Sri Lanka

Population (2019)	21,324,000
Over 60 years of age (%)[a]	3,397,000 (15.9%)
Density	325 inhabitants/km^2
Ethnic groups	
Sinhalese	74.9%
Sri Lankan Tamil	11.2%
Indian Tamil	4.1%
Sri Lankan Moors	9.3%
Other	0.5%
Religion	
Buddhism	70.1%
Hinduism	12.6%
Islam	9.7%
Roman Catholic	6.2%
Christianity	1.4%
Geography	Southern Asia, island in the Indian Ocean
Climate	Tropical monsoon
Government	Democratic Socialist Republic of Sri Lanka
Literacy rate, 2018 (15 years and older)[b]	91.71%
Economy (2018)[c]	
GDP, PPP	$291.9 billion
GDP per capita, PPP	$13,473
GDP	$88.9 billion
GDP per capita	$4,102
Major income sources	Services, textiles, tourism, agricultural products (paddy, tea, rubber, coconut, etc.)
Female participation in paid workforce (2018)[d]	33.6%
Urbanization[c]	18.5%
Net migration (2018)[d]	−4.6% per 1,000 population
Maternal mortality ratio (2015)[e]	30 per 100,000 births
Major historical events	Independence: 1948 Economic liberalization: 1977 Civil unrest: 1983–2009 Tsunami: 2004

GDP = gross domestic product, km^2 = square kilometer, PPP = purchasing power parity.

[a] Calculation based on United Nations. 2019. *World Population Prospects: The 2019 Revision*. New York.
[b] Taken from UNESCO UIS http://uis.unesco.org/en/country/lk (accessed 3 April 2020).
[c] World Bank. World Development Indicators. https://databank.worldbank.org/source/world-development-indicators (accessed 9 April 2020).
[d] Asian Development Bank. Key Indicators Database: Sri Lanka. https://kidb.adb.org/kidb/sdbsCountryView/countryViewResult ?selectedCountryId=190&selectedCountryShortName= (accessed 9 April 2020).
[e] World Health Organization. Global Health Expenditure Database. https://apps.who.int/nha/database (accessed 8 April 2020).

Sources: Central Bank of Sri Lanka. Annual Report 2016; Government of Sri Lanka, Department of Census and Statistics. 2012. *Census of Population and Housing: Sri Lanka 2012;* World Bank. World Development Indicators; Asian Development Bank. Key Indicators; United Nations. 2019. *World Population Prospects: The 2019 Revision;* and UNESCO Institute of Statistics.

II. METHODS

Following an international literature review and development of a country diagnostic framework and methodology draft, the international team and national consultants agreed to the methodology for the country diagnostic study (CDS) in January 2017 at a workshop with the Asian Development Bank regional technical assistance 9111 team.

The CDS team conducted a gap analysis to identify available data, data sources, and gaps in information. The first stakeholder meeting was held in Colombo on 9 February 2017 to gather information for the gap analysis and begin the consultative process. The meeting was attended by officers from the Ministry of Social Empowerment and Welfare; the Ministry of National Policies and Economic Affairs; the Ministry of Health, Nutrition and Indigenous Medicine; United Nations agencies; academics; nongovernment organizations (NGOs); the National Secretariat for Elders (NSE); the Sri Lanka Medical Association; the Sri Lanka Association of Geriatric Medicine; and private sector LTC service providers.

Healthy and Active Ageing in Sri Lanka, by Wendy Holmes, was used as a starting point for the desk research for this study.[7] This was complemented by searches in digital libraries of scholarly articles and a search for small-scale research and surveys in the Postgraduate Institute of Medicine (PGIM) library. Digital libraries (e.g., Pubmed, Google Scholar, and Hinari) were searched using the following search terms: Sri Lanka elders, Sri Lanka LTC, Sri Lanka long-term care, Sri Lanka ADL, Sri Lanka activities of daily living, Sri Lanka living arrangements, and Sri Lanka co-residence.

Key informant interviews (KIIs) were conducted to obtain additional information on areas with data gaps. Seven KIIs were carried out with officials from the NSE; then Directorate for Youth, Elderly and Disabled Persons; the Ministry of Health (YED MOH); NGOs; other government officials; and academics involved in training human resources for LTC for older persons. Key informants represented government agencies and NGOs involved or interested in LTC. KII questions covered understanding the care needs of older people; understanding the supply of care, regulatory, and policy framework; and LTC service provision, LTC quality management, and LTC human resources and financing. Appendix 1 summarizes the KIIs.

Group consultations were held at three levels: provincial, district, and divisional. Sri Lanka has 9 provinces and 25 districts. The consultations gathered information on the responsibilities of on-the-ground health and social service officers and any challenges they face or anticipate in providing LTC for elders. Comparing information from provincial, district, and divisional levels within the same province showed how these three levels are coordinated and monitored, given that administration and programs may differ from province to province.

The divisional-level group consultation was held in Padukka, a rural area in Colombo district, with staff from the Padukkan Medical Officer of Health and social development officers from the Department of

---

7   W. Holmes. 2015. *Healthy and Active Ageing in Sri Lanka: A Register of Relevant Research Publications and Presentations.*

Social Services working in Padukka. The district-level group consultation was held with officers from the Office for the Regional Director of Health Services in Colombo. The provincial-level group consultation was held with provincial-level officers at the Office of the Provincial Director of Health Services, Western Province. Western Province and Colombo district were selected due to time and financial constraints faced by the team.

A focus group discussion was held with a group of 12 able elders in the Padukka area. This discussion gathered information on the social problems people face in old age, problems faced by families when providing LTC, and the kind of support they receive from members of the community.

No accurate data were available on the nature of services provided by eldercare homes and in-home nursing care services in Sri Lanka. To circumvent this lack of information, the CDS team conducted a national survey of eldercare homes (for-profit and not-for-profit) and in-home nursing care services. The surveys received ethical clearance from the Institutional Review Board of the Institute for Health Policy (IHP).

The sampling frame for not-for-profit eldercare homes was from the list of registered institutions available from the NSE. The sampling frame for in-home nursing care services was obtained from the MOH. We identified an incomplete list of 227 not-for-profit and 13 for-profit homes in the 2016 report on LTC in Sri Lanka by the United Nations Economic and Social Commission for Asia and the Pacific,[8] so others were added and surveyed to learn more. The final sampling frames were compiled from lists obtained from the NSE, MOH, and IHP, and attained by searches in the telephone directory and the Google search engine.

The total sampling frame consisted of institutions from all nine provinces. Additionally, the sampling frames comprised 260 institutions for eldercare homes and 24 institutions for in-home nursing care services. All institutions were surveyed, mainly through a postal survey and complemented by a reminder telephone call, reminder mail, and field visits by the CDS team and district officers from the Ministry of Social Empowerment and Welfare. The response rates were 70% from eldercare homes and 25% from in-home nursing care services. In-home nursing care services were reluctant to reveal business information as for-profit institutions, and they have no legal obligation to respond to the NSE because they are registered with the MOH. Results presented in the report are estimated based on the responses received.

Data from the World Bank 2006 Sri Lanka Aging Survey, the Census of Population and Housing 2012/2013, the Household Income and Expenditure Survey 2016, and the Labor Force Surveys 1996–2014 were analyzed to obtain population data, data on living arrangements, ability to perform activities of daily living (ADL) and instrumental activities of daily living (IADL), and the disability and mobility of older people in Sri Lanka.

The World Bank 2006 Sri Lanka Aging Survey was based on a representative sample of 2,413 Sri Lankans aged 60+ years in 13 out of 17 districts. The northeastern provinces were excluded due to civil unrest in the area at the time of the survey. Data collection included up to three interviews in each household with (i) the selected older person, (ii) one adult child (over 15 years old), and (iii) the household head or the most knowledgeable person (footnote 4).

A 10-person working group (comprised of stakeholders from government, private, academic, and NGO sectors) was formed to advise and review the CDS process. This working group met three times during the study to review the work and provide inputs.

In early 2020, some of the data cited in this report were updated to latest available.

---

[8]   W. Holmes. 2016. *Long-Term Care of Older Persons in Sri Lanka*. Bangkok: UNESCAP.

III. FINDINGS

A. Understanding the Care Needs of Older Persons

1. Demography

The population of Sri Lanka increased from 16.5 million in 1990 to 21.3 million by 2019.[9] In contrast, population growth rate has declined over time, reaching 1.0% in 2018.[10] The population density was 346 persons per square kilometer in 2018, one of the highest in the world.[11]

Table 1: People Aged 60 Years and Older, 1990–2050
(%)

Age (years)	1990	2000	2015	2030	2050
60–69	4.7	5.6	9.2	10.1	11.2
70–79	2.4	3.1	5.1	6.7	8.9
80+	0.8	1.0	1.6	2.5	5.1
Total	7.9	9.7	15.9	19.4	25.2

Sources: IHP estimates by A.T.P.L. Abeykoon based on the Census of Population and Housing by the Department of Census and Statistics 1981, 2001, and 2012; and population growth and long-term population projections for Sri Lanka 2015–2115 by A.T.P.L. Abeykoon and I. de Silva. 2016. (unpublished); Calculation based on United Nations. 2019. *World Population Prospects: The 2019 Revision*. New York.

In 2019, approximately 15.9% of the population of Sri Lanka was older than 60 years of age, with 9.2% aged 60–69 years, 5.1% aged 70–79 years, and 1.6% over 80 years of age (Table 1). Projections suggest that these proportions will increase, more than doubling between 2030 and 2050; 60% will be women (Table 2). This also represents a significant increase in absolute numbers as the total population increases from between 1990 and 2050.

---

[9] Calculation based on United Nations. 2019. *World Population Prospects: The 2019 Revision*.

[10] World Bank. World Development Indicators. https://databank.worldbank.org/source/world-development-indicators (accessed 9 April 2020).

[11] Asian Development Bank. Key Indicators Database: Sri Lanka. https://kidb.adb.org/kidb/sdbsCountryView/countryViewResult ?selectedCountryId=190&selectedCountryShortName= (accessed 9 April 2020).

Table 2: People Aged 60 Years and Older by Age Group and Sex, 1990–2050

Age (years)	1990		2000		2015		2030		2050	
	Male	Female	Male	Female	Male	Female	Male	Female	Male	Female
60–69	4.9	4.6	5.5	5.6	7.2	8.0	9.8	10.4	10.1	12.3
70–79	2.4	2.3	3.1	3.1	3.0	3.8	6.1	7.3	7.1	10.8
80+	0.8	0.8	1.0	1.0	1.1	1.6	1.9	3.1	3.8	6.5
Total	8.1	7.6	9.6	9.8	11.3	13.4	17.8	20.8	21.0	29.6

Sources: IHP estimates by A.T.P.L. Abeykoon based on Census of Population and Housing by the Department of Census and Statistics 1981, 2001, and 2012; and population growth and long-term population projections for Sri Lanka 2015-2115 by A.T.P.L. Abeykoon and I. de Silva. 2016. (unpublished).

The Sri Lankan population is expected to undergo major changes in its age structure in the coming decades.[12] Population age–sex pyramids demonstrate a shift from a large proportion of young people to a large proportion of older people (Figure 1). The pyramids also indicate that older age groups will have a larger proportion of women. Projections suggest that the carrying capacity (i.e., the maximum population size that the ecosystem can support) would be 25 million during the 2050s. Higher than predicted fertility among teenagers and women aged 35–49 years will likely contribute to a more gradual transition to an aging population, at least in the coming decade; mortality and migration will contribute to a much lesser extent (footnote 4).

The "old-age dependency ratio" (i.e., proportion of those older than 60 years compared to the working-age population of 15–59 years) is projected to rise steadily, from 20% in 2015 to 43% in 2050.[13] In reality, many elders older than 60 years are not dependent, financially or otherwise, and continue to contribute to their families and the economy by undertaking domestic work, childcare, and work in the informal sector.[14]

Life expectancy at birth has increased for males and females and likely will continue to increase (Table 3). The speed of population aging (i.e., the number of years it would take for the proportion of the population aged 65+ years to move from 7% to 14% of the total population) was 20 years in 2007.

2. Older People's Situation

In Sri Lanka, people in formal employment usually retire at 55–60 years of age, but some continue to perform paid work at a much older age depending on economic level, health status, and preference. The labor force participation rate is 22.5% among people aged 65+ years (38% among men and 10% among women).[15] After retiring, many elders look after their grandchildren and engage in social, cultural, and religious activities. Many elders also continue to work in the informal sector.

[12] A.T.P.L. Abeykoon and I. de Silva. 2016. Long-Term Population Projections for Sri Lanka 2015–2115. Colombo, Sri Lanka: Institute for Health Policy. Unpublished.
[13] Asian Development Bank. 2019. *Growing Old Before Becoming Rich: Challenges of an Aging Population in Sri Lanka.* Manila.
[14] S.T. Hettige. 2014. Social Integration, Sustainable Livelihood, and Social Protection of Elders in Sri Lanka. In Human Rights Commission of Sri Lanka and HelpAge Sri Lanka, eds. *Growing Old Gracefully.* Sri Lanka: HRCSL. pp. 57–72.
[15] Government of Sri Lanka, Department of Census and Statistics. 2015. *Sri Lanka Labour Force Survey Annual Report 2015.* Sri Lanka: Department of Census and Statistics.

Figure 1: Population Pyramids for Sri Lanka, 2015–2115
(%)

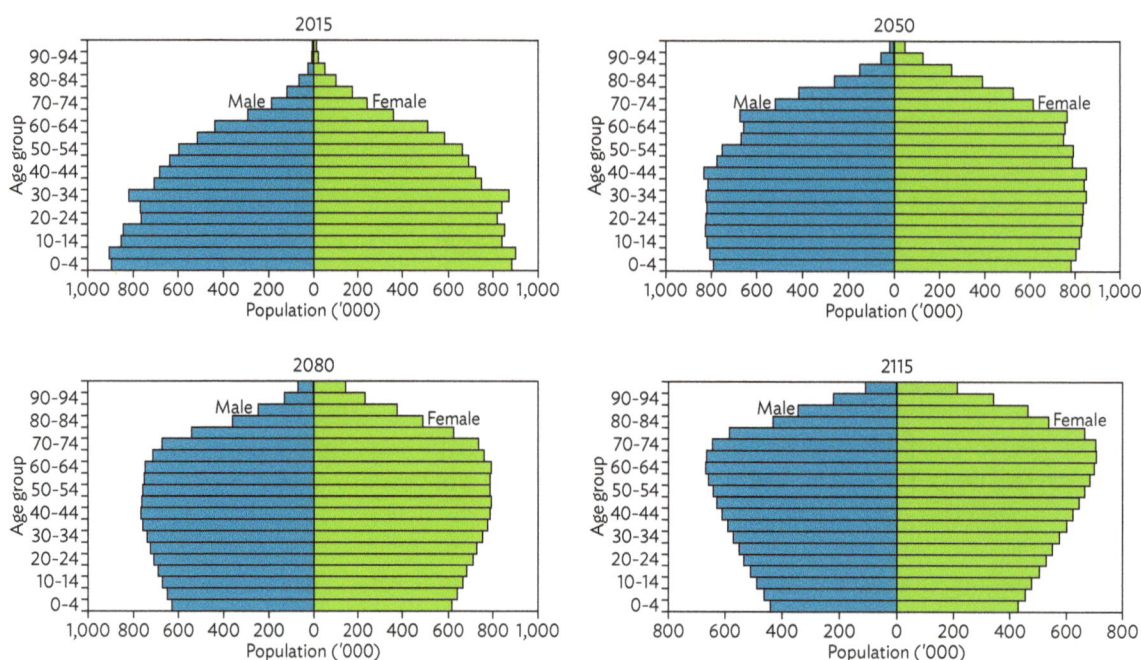

Source: Long-term population projections for Sri Lanka 2015-2115 by A.T.P.L. Abeykoon and I. de Silva. 2016. (unpublished).

Table 3: Life Expectancy and Healthy Life Expectancy by Sex, 1990–2050

	1990	2000	2010	2015	2030	2050
Life expectancy at birth (years)						
Males	68	69	72	73	74	77
Females	74	76	78	79	80	82
Life expectancy at age 60 (years)						
Males	18	18	18	19	19	21
Females	21	22	22	22	23	23
Healthy life expectancy at birth (years)						
Males	...	61	...	64[a]	...	...
Females	...	67	...	70[a]	...	...
Healthy life expectancy at age 60 (years)						
Males	...	14	...	15[a]	...	...
Females	...	16	...	17[a]	...	...

... = data not available.

[a] Data for the year 2016.

Sources: Life tables for Sri Lanka 2011–2013, Department of Census and Statistics and author's calculations using long-term population projections for Sri Lanka 2015–2115 by A.T.P.L. Abeykoon and I. de Silva. 2016. (unpublished); and WHO. 2016. Global Health Estimates Summary Tables (accessed 6 March 2017).

Pensions and old-age income. Sri Lanka has seven different types of old-age income schemes: (i) the Civil Pensions Scheme, (ii) the Employees' Provident Fund, (iii) the Employees' Trust Fund, (iv) the Farmers' Pension and Social Security Benefit Scheme, (v) the Fishermen's Pension and Social Security Benefit Scheme, (vi) the Pension and Social Security Benefit Scheme for Self-Employed Persons, and (vii) the recently introduced "Wadihiti Saviyata Jeshta Purawasi Deemanawa" (Senior Citizen's Allowance) program. However, the Employees' Provident Fund and Employees' Trust Fund are not categorized as pension schemes, because the payout is made in a lump sum, thus limiting the availability of a regular income.

In total, Sri Lanka spent about 3% of its gross domestic product (GDP) on these schemes in 2016, and the level of expenditure has not changed significantly. In 2016, about 38% of the population older than 60 years was covered by one of the five pension schemes (footnote 13). Prior to the introduction of the "Wadihiti Saviyata Jeshta Purawasi Deemanawa" (Senior Citizen's Allowance) program in 2013, coverage was just 22%. This program delivers benefits of SLRs2,000 (about $12) per month to people over the age of 70 years whose monthly income is less than SLRs3,000.[16]

Living Arrangements. Findings from the World Bank 2006 Sri Lanka Aging Survey, the National Survey on Elders 2003–2004, and multiple other small studies suggest that older people's living arrangements have not changed much over time.[17] Many elders live with their spouses and/or adult children. Very few live independently, but their numbers are increasing.[18]

The 2006 World Bank survey found that 38% of older people lived with their spouse and adult children and 38% lived with adult children. Of the respondents, 9.5% lived with their spouse only, while just 5.2% lived alone (Table 4). Most older persons who reported living alone were women. There are no age- and sex-disaggregated data on widowhood, and a limited number of existing national surveys (e.g., the Demographic and Health Survey) only include marital status for women of reproductive age; the 2006 Sri Lanka Ageing Report does not include sex disaggregation for marital status. It does highlight that there are more widowed women than men, because widowhood is common among women older than 70 years and there are more older women than older men.

A more recent survey of three Medical Officer of Health areas in Badulla, Kandaketiya, and Passara shows that 34% of older persons live with their spouse and children and almost 32% with their children (Table 4).[19] The percentage of those living with just their spouses was about 24%, while only 6.2% reported living alone. Similar to the 2006 survey, the majority of those who reported living alone were women.

The urban, rural, and estate sectors appear to show a slight variation in older persons' living arrangements[20] (Table 5). The proportion of elders living alone was higher in the estate sector than in the other sectors.

The report on the national survey of 2006 suggests a trend whereby older people initially live with their spouse or with spouse and children, but can no longer support themselves independently when their spouse dies and so live

---

[16] Author calculations based on data provided to the Institute for Health Policy (IHP) from the Department of Pensions, the Agricultural and Agrarian Insurance Board, and the Social Security Board of Sri Lanka.

[17] S. Rathnayake and S. Siop. 2015. Quality of Life and Its Determinants Among Older People Living in the Rural Community in Sri Lanka. *Indian Journal of Gerontology.* 29 (2). pp. 131-153; and M. H. Watt, B. Perera, T. Østbye, S. Ranabahu, H. Rajapakse, and J. Maselko. 2014. Caregiving Expectations and Challenges among Elders and Their Adult Children in Southern Sri Lanka. *Ageing and Society.* 34 (5). pp. 838–858.

[18] K. A. P. Siddhisena. 2014. *Ageing Population and Aged Care in Sri Lanka: An Overview.* Australian Demographic and Social Research Institute, 30-05-2014; and T.K. Silva. 2004. Elderly Population, Family Support and Intergenerational Arrangements. *Ageing Population in Sri Lanka.* Colombo, Sri Lanka: PASL and UNFPA.

[19] Directorate for Youth, Elderly and Disabled Persons, Ministry of Health. 2016. Report on the institutional survey and community survey in selected areas of Sri Lanka on older people's healthcare.

[20] An estate sector consists of all plantations that are 20 acres or more and have 10 or more resident laborers.

Table 4: Living Arrangements of Older People by Sex, 2006 and 2016
(%)

Living Arrangements	2006			2016		
	Male	Female	Total	Male	Female	Total
Alone	2.9	6.9	5.2	1.8	9.2	6.2
With spouse only	14.6	5.4	9.5	30.7	18.8	23.6
With spouse and adult child	60.0	20.7	38.1	48.5	24.5	34.1
With adult children only	15.0	57.1	38.5	16.0	42.0	31.6
Other living arrangement	3.9	2.2	2.9	1.2	4.5	3.2
Not answered	3.5	7.7	5.9	1.8	1.0	1.3
Total	100.0	100.0	100.0	100.0	100.0	100.0

Sources: Author's calculations based on World Bank. 2006. Sri Lanka Aging Survey; and Directorate for Youth, Elderly and Disabled Persons, Ministry of Health. 2016. Report on the institutional survey and community survey in selected areas of Sri Lanka on older people's healthcare.

Table 5: Living Arrangements of Older People by Sector, 2006 and 2016
(%)

Living Arrangements	2006			2016		
	Urban	Rural	Estate	Urban	Rural	Estate
Alone	2.9	5.8	10.9	4.2	5.5	5.6
With spouse only	8.0	10.2	9.3	19.1	27.2	25.5
With spouse and adult child	36.9	38.6	38.8	39.5	29.4	32.7
With adult children only	40.9	37.7	34.1	31.5	32.2	30.6
Other living arrangement	2.3	3.1	3.9	4.2	2.0	3.6
Not answered	9.0	4.6	3.1	1.5	0.7	2.0
Total	100.0	100.0	100.0	100.0	97.0	100.0

Sources: Author's calculations based on World Bank. 2006. Sri Lanka Aging Survey; and Directorate for Youth, Elderly and Disabled Persons, Ministry of Health. 2016. Report on the institutional survey and community survey in selected areas of Sri Lanka on older people's healthcare.

with their adult children (footnote 5). Figure 2 shows that the likelihood of elders living with their adult children increases with age. This trend is mostly observable among older women because they live longer than men.

The analysis of the Labor Force Surveys 1996–2014 showed a slight increase in the number of older people who live alone. Interestingly, there also appeared to be an increase in the number of households where people older than 75 years live in households with other similarly aged residents (Figure 3). These trends are similar to those in Japan in 1960–1975 (Figure 3). In their study on a selected rural community in Sri Lanka, Rathnayake and Siop (2015) found that the living arrangements of older persons significantly affect quality of life: those who lived alone tended to have a poorer quality of life compared to those who lived with spouses and/or children or others. Since living alone is linked to loneliness and poorer mental health, it is important to pay attention to this fact.[21]

---

[21]   R. Fukunaga, et al. 2012. Living Alone Is Associated with Depression among the Elderly in a Rural Community in Japan. *Psychogeriatrics, The Official Journal of the Japanese Psychogeriatrics Society*. 12 (3). pp. 179–185.

Figure 2: Living Arrangements of Older Persons by Age and Sex, 2006

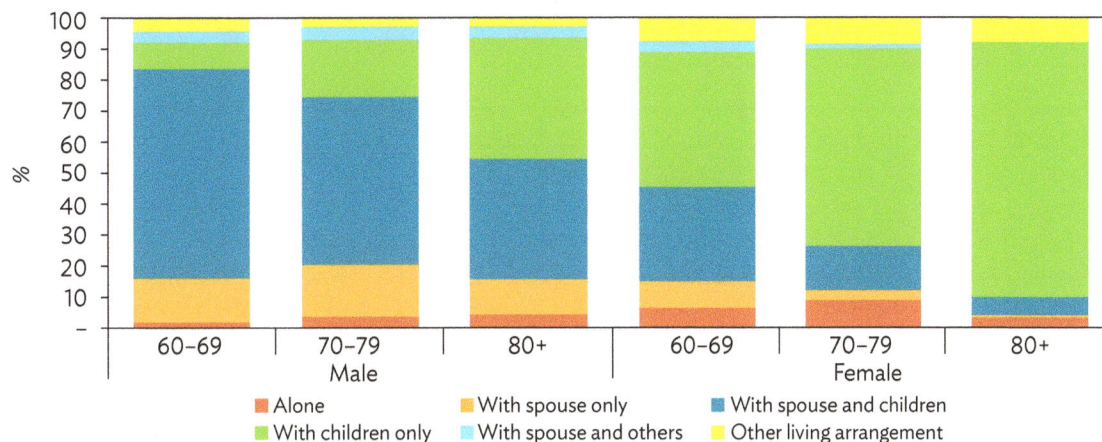

Legend:
- Alone
- With spouse only
- With spouse and children
- With children only
- With spouse and others
- Other living arrangement

Source: Author's calculations based on World Bank. 2006. Sri Lanka Aging Survey.

Figure 3: Trends in Living Arrangements of Older Persons in Sri Lanka and Japan

(a) Trends in living arrangements of older persons in Sri Lanka, 1996–2014

(b) Trends in living arrangements of older persons in Sri Lanka and Japan

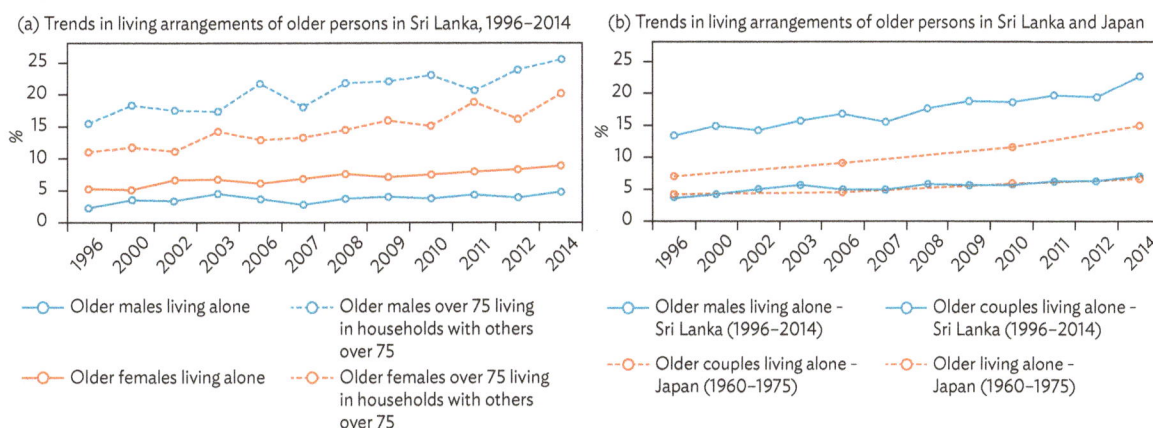

Legend (a):
- Older males living alone
- Older males over 75 living in households with others over 75
- Older females living alone
- Older females over 75 living in households with others over 75

Legend (b):
- Older males living alone - Sri Lanka (1996–2014)
- Older couples living alone - Sri Lanka (1996–2014)
- Older couples living alone - Japan (1960–1975)
- Older living alone - Japan (1960–1975)

Sources: Author's analysis of Labor Force Surveys Sri Lanka 1996–2014; and H. Kojima. 1995. *Population Aging and Living Arrangements of the Elderly in Japan*.

3.   Health and Disability

Although most older people remain well, many experience a decline in intrinsic capacity as they age, due to chronic diseases, injuries, or cognitive decline that inhibits their ability to live independently (i.e., without support). In 2016, life expectancy in Sri Lanka at age 60 was 19 years for men and 22 years for women, but healthy life expectancy was estimated at 15 years for men and 17 years for women (Table 3). There is debate globally on whether the average period of morbidity in old age will decrease as life expectancies increase—the "compression of morbidity"—or whether greater life expectancy will give older people a longer period of living in poor health, with a resulting increase in need for LTC.

Asking about ability to undertake activities of daily living (ADL) and instrumental activities of daily living (IADL) is commonly used as a way to assess the need for care and support among older persons. Unfortunately, Sri Lanka has little nationally representative data on frequency of needing assistance with ADL and IADL. In general, older people are more likely to need assistance with IADL than ADL, those over 80 years of age are more likely to need assistance, and older women are more likely to need help than older men according to World Bank's 2006 national survey on aging (Table 6). However, a 2016 survey by the Directorate for Youth, Elderly and Disabled Persons in the Medical Officer of Health areas of Badulla, Kandaketiya, and Passara (Table 7) and a smaller study of older people's ability to perform ADL found less variation between the sexes.[22] In general, more physically demanding activities (e.g., walking and getting in and out of a bed or chair) require assistance more frequently than eating and dressing. However, the level of physical demand likely depends on the setting. For example, some older people have a walk-in shower, while others use a step-in-bath or bathe at a well or in a river. Additionally, methodological differences between studies may affect findings (e.g., whether housebound elders are included in the sample interviewed, whether fitter elders are missed because they work, and whether those with cognitive decline are excluded or have a family member to answer for them).

The 2006 World Bank study reported the prevalence of difficulties with ADL and IADL as age increases: about 35%–40% of people older than 80 years had difficulty with at least two ADLs (Figure 4). Fernando and Seneviratna (1993) also found a consistent decrease in self-evaluated health as age increases. The most commonly reported health problems in their study were arthritis, high blood pressure, and heart and lung diseases.

Table 6: Inability to Perform Activities of Daily Living and Instrumental Activities of Daily Living by Age and Sex
(%)

Activity	60–69		70–79		80+	
	Male	Female	Male	Female	Male	Female
ADL						
Unable to eat without assistance	2.1	0.8	4.2	5.3	16.8	18.1
Unable to dress without help	2.2	1.3	5.0	8.0	18.6	23.3
Unable to use toilet without help	3.8	2.7	6.2	11.2	26.5	30.6
Unable to bathe without help	5.8	6.5	10.6	22.0	44.2	52.8
Unable to stand up from sitting on a chair without help	6.2	10.5	13.4	24.5	38.1	49.2
IADL						
Unable to prepare meals	10.6	7.0	22.4	28.2	60.2	60.1
Unable to take medication	4.1	5.3	10.1	18.0	37.2	43.5
Unable to shop for or obtain food from usual source	6.0	9.1	13.7	29.0	50.4	66.3
Unable to manage money/finances	4.8	5.4	7.8	20.6	31.0	48.2
Unable to sweep floor or yard	6.9	7.8	17.1	24.3	53.1	55.4

ADL = activities of daily living, IADL = instrumental activities of daily living.

Note: Respondents who reported "have trouble performing" and "unable to perform" were judged unable perform the task without assistance.

Source: Author's calculations based on World Bank. 2006. Sri Lanka Aging Survey.

---

[22]   D. N. Fernando and R. de A. Seneviratna. 1993. Physical Health and Functional Ability of an Elderly Population in Sri Lanka. *The Ceylon Journal of Medical Science.* 36 (1). pp. 9–16.

Table 7: Inability to Perform Activities of Daily Living by Sex, 2016
(%)

Activity	Sex		Total
	Male	Female	
Unable to dress without help	13.3	13.8	13.6
Unable to eat without assistance	12.0	13.2	12.7
Unable to walk without assistance	16.3	19.7	18.3
Unable to use toilet without help	14.5	15.3	15.0
Unable to brush teeth without help	9.3	11.7	10.7
Unable to get on and off bed without help	11.5	13.3	12.6
Unable to wash clothes without help	21.5	19.7	20.4

Note: All survey respondents were elders aged 60+ years.

Source: Directorate for Youth, Elderly and Disabled Persons, Ministry of Health. 2016. Report on the institutional survey and community survey in selected areas of Sri Lanka on older people's healthcare.

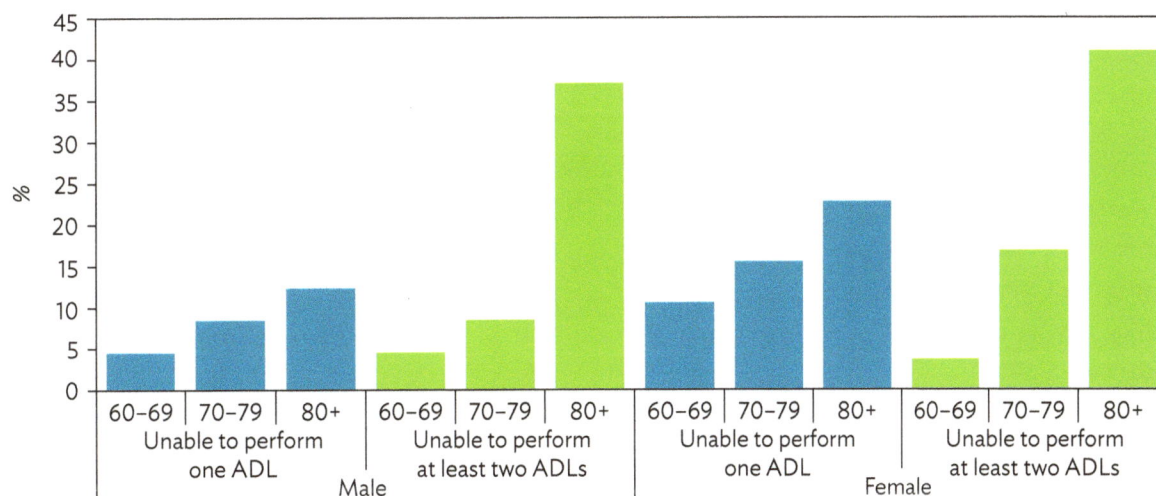

Figure 4: Inability to Perform Activities by Age and Sex, 2006
(%)

ADL = activities of daily living.

Source: Author's calculations based on World Bank. 2006. Sri Lanka Aging Survey.

WHO-SAGE Wave 1 data from the People's Republic of China, South Africa, the Russian Federation, and India show the frequency of difficulty with ADL, and the author's calculations of ADL deficiency in Sri Lanka from the 2006 World Bank study (Figure 5). Sri Lanka appears to be on the lower range of both one and more than two ADL deficiencies.

Figure 5: Age-Standardized Prevalence of Deficiency in Activities of Daily Living in Adults >50 Years

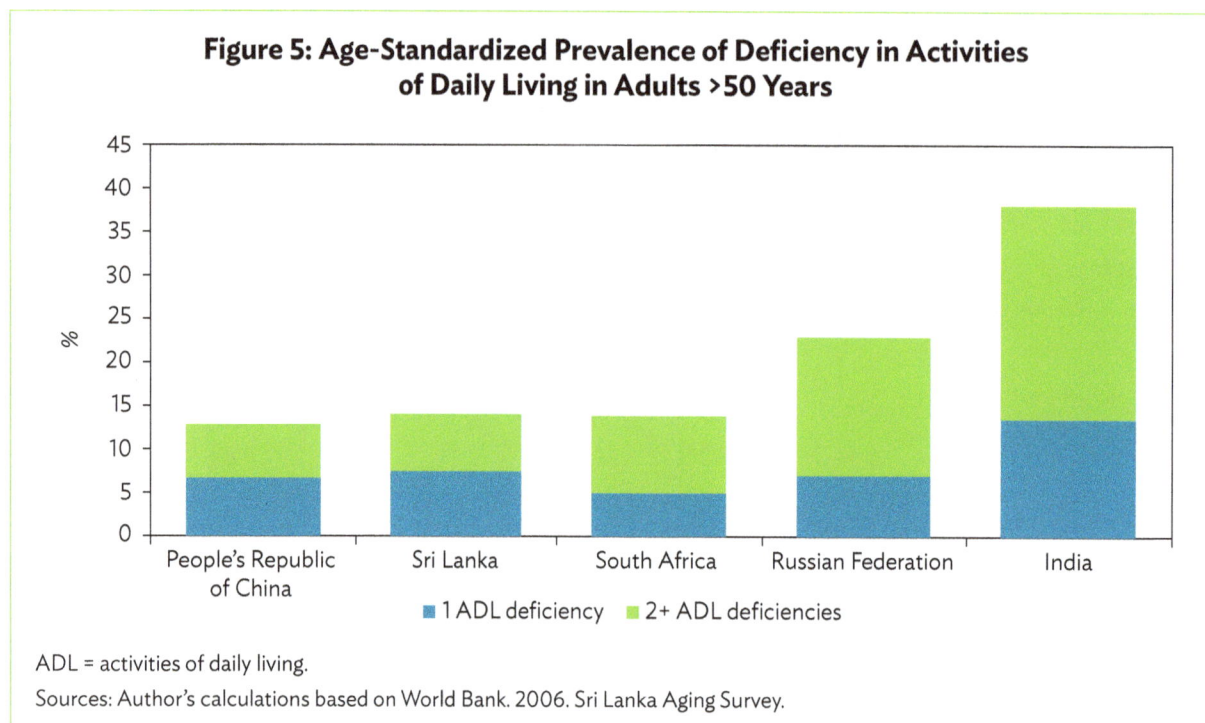

ADL = activities of daily living.
Sources: Author's calculations based on World Bank. 2006. Sri Lanka Aging Survey.

Table 8: Population Facing a Disability and/or Difficulty by Age and Sex, 2012
(%)

Type of Difficulty	60–69		70–79		80+		
	Male	Female	Male	Female	Male	Female	Total
Vision (even with the use of eyeglasses)	15.4	17.3	26.2	30.2	37.9	41.2	22.2
Hearing (even with the use of hearing aids)	5.3	5.5	16.1	17.4	33.1	34.9	11.6
Walking	9.8	13.8	23.0	30.3	41.8	50.6	19.9
Cognition	3.4	4.5	9.7	12.9	23.3	29.8	8.5
Self-care	1.8	1.8	5.9	6.8	15.4	22.6	5.0
Communication	1.6	1.5	3.7	4.1	9.6	12.2	3.2

Source: Author's calculations based on the Government of Sri Lanka, Department of Census and Statistics. 2012. *Census of Population and Housing: Sri Lanka 2012; 5% Provisional Sample.*

Variation is slight between the rural and estate sectors, but the prevalence of vision difficulties seems lower in the urban sector compared to the rural and estate sectors (Table 8). In part, this reflects a lack of access to eye-care services (e.g., cataract surgery and provision of spectacles) in rural and estate settings[23] (Table 9). Vision impairment is common among elders and a major reason for needing LTC services, increasing the risk

---

[23] *National Survey of Blindness, Visual Impairment, Ocular Morbidity and Disability in Sri Lanka: A Report.* 2014-2015; Vision 2020 secretariat, Ministry of Health Sri Lanka; and International Centre for Eye Health Department of Clinical Research, Faculty of Infectious and Tropical Diseases, London School of Hygiene and Tropical Medicine. London, United Kingdom. https://www.iapb.org/learn/resources/national-survey-of-blindness-and-vi-sri-lanka-2014-15/.

Table 9: Elder Population Aged 60 Years and Older Facing a Disability and/or Difficulty by Sector, 2012

(%)

Type of Difficulty	Sector			Total
	Urban	Rural	Estate	
Vision (even with the use of eyeglasses)	17.2	23.3	23.5	22.2
Hearing (even with the use of hearing aids)	8.1	12.5	9.6	11.6
Walking	16.5	20.5	20.7	19.9
Cognition	6.7	9.0	7.1	8.5
Self-care	4.3	5.1	4.1	5.0
Communication	2.7	3.3	2.8	3.2

Source: Author's calculations based on Government of Sri Lanka, Department of Census and Statistics. 2012. *Census of Population and Housing: Sri Lanka 2012*; 5% Provisional Sample.

of isolation, depression, injuries from falls, reducing access to health-care facilities, and making it difficult to read health information or take medicines. However, most vision impairment in this age group results from cataract or refractive error, which can be easily and cheaply treated. Reducing the need for LTC services requires strengthening the eye-care system.[24]

Table 10 examines the prevalence rates of selected noncommunicable diseases reported in several studies conducted in Sri Lanka. Stroke prevalence is higher among men in all older age groups, while diabetes and dementia are higher among women than men in all older age groups. Over half of older adults have hypertension and around a quarter have diabetes. Both conditions are often undetected and untreated.[25]

4.   Demand for Care

According to key government informants, the need for care among older persons has increased. Since people are living longer, physical and mental conditions related to age are becoming more prevalent, increasing the need for care. On the other hand, care provision has remained mainly with families, and formal LTC service provision is considered inadequate to meet even current needs and demand. Key informants from government, NGOs, and professional bodies consider LTC services for elders extremely inadequate. Despite this wide gap between the need for care and its provision, few groups or organizations demand better and more adequate LTC services.

When key informants were asked if policymakers understand the need for formal and dedicated LTC services in old age, their reaction was mixed. Some felt that policymakers have shown some understanding of this need, while others were not convinced. On the other hand, the informants felt that government officials were more aware of the need for LTC services than politicians.

[24] *Actions to Address the Growing Burden of Avoidable Blindness among Elders in Sri Lanka*. 2016. The Fred Hollows Foundation; Burnet Institute; National Secretariat for Elders; PALM Foundation; Sarvodaya; Plantation Human Development Trust; Berendina Development Services. https://www.burnet.edu.au/system/asset/file/2160/8._Policy_brief_web.pdf.

[25] A. Kasturiratne, T. Warnakulasuriya, J. Pinidiyapathirage, et al. 2011. P2-130 Epidemiology of Hypertension in an Urban Sri Lankan Population. *Journal of Epidemiology & Community Health*. 2011;65:A256; and P. Katulanda et al. 2008. Prevalence and Projections of Diabetes and Pre-Diabetes in Adults in Sri Lanka—Sri Lanka Diabetes. Cardiovascular Study (SLDCS). *Diabetic Medicine*. 25 (9). pp. 1062–1069.

Table 10: Prevalence of Selected Noncommunicable Diseases by Age Group and Sex, 2005–2015 (%)

Condition	Data Source	Definition	Year	Male 60–69 (years)			Female 60–69 (years)		
Heart disease	WHO STEPS (2015)[a]	Self-reported heart attack or chest pain	2014–2015	14.6	...	...	9.8	...	...
	Katulanda, IHP analysis	Diagnosis card or self-reported diagnoses of ischemic heart disease	2005–2006	4.1	7.2	13.3	6.2	2.8	11.9
Stroke	Katulanda, IHP analysis	Diagnosis card or self-reported diagnoses of cerebrovascular disease	2005–2006	6.5	9.6	4.2	3.2	2.5	5.9
Hypertension	WHO STEPS (2015)[a]	BP ≥ 140/90, or taking antihypertensive	2014–2015	47.8	...	...	66.4	...	...
	The prevalence, predictors and associations of hypertension in Sri Lanka: a cross-sectional population based national survey[c]	BP ≥ 140/90, or taking antihypertensive, or previously diagnosed	2005–2006	52.8	59.7	...	48.6	68.5	...
	Katulanda, IHP analysis	BP ≥ 140/90, or taking antihypertensive	2005–2006	51.2	58.0	65.7	44.8	63.6	49.4
Diabetes	Prevalence and projections of diabetes and pre-diabetes in adults in Sri Lanka—Sri Lanka Diabetes, Cardiovascular Study (SLDCS)[b]	Diagnosed diabetes (verified by medical records, laboratory reports, prescriptions), and/or FPG ≥ 7 mmol/L or 2 hr post OGTT ≥ 11.1 mmol/L	2005–2006	18.1	22.9	...	24.2	24.0	...
	Katulanda, IHP analysis	FPG >= 126mg/dL, taking medication, or OGTT >=11.1 mmol/L	2005–2006	21.6	21.9	10.6	25.8	23.4	26.0
Dementia	Prevalence of dementia in a semi-urban population in Sri Lanka: report from a regional survey[c]	Structured assessment, physical and neurological examination, blood tests, and CT scans	2000–2001	3.0	5.0	...	3.4	10.4	12.5
	Prevalence and correlates of clinically significant depressive symptoms among older people in Sri Lanka: findings from a national survey[d]	Geriatric Depression Scale-15 score >= 16	2006	19.1	27.1	23.1	25.3	36.0	30.7

... = data not available, BP = blood pressure, CT = computer tomography, FPG = fasting plasma glucose, IHP = Institute for Health Policy, mmol/L = millimoles per liter, OGTT = oral glucose tolerance test, WHO STEPS = WHO STEPwise Approach to Surveillance.

Notes:
[a] STEPS survey did not cover those ≥70 years.
[b] Data entered in 70–79-year age group is actually for 70+ years. Standardized to WHO 2005 population. Diabetes prevalence from the most recent STEPS survey (2015) are not included, as there has been debate about the accuracy of the results; another STEPS survey is being planned with a change in the equipment used to measure blood glucose.
[c] Survey in Ragama of 703 adults over the age of 65. Age groups reported are different: 65–75, 76–85, >85. These have been included in the age group 5 years below.
[d] Data from Sri Lanka Aging Survey of 1,181 participants, aged 60 and older.

Sources: Ministry of Health, Nutrition and Indigenous Medicine. 2015; Rannan-Eliya et al. 2010; Katulanda et al. 2008; Katulanda et al. 2014; Silva, Gunatilake, and Smith. 2003; Malhotra, Chan, and Østbye. 2010; and IHP analysis of Sri Lanka Diabetes and Cardiovascular Survey.

However, the general public was thought to be unaware of the need for formal LTC services in old age, probably because people only become aware of such need when they are sensitized to the issue through personal experience, although as need increases, demand could be expected to increase as well. Greater awareness of an integrated LTC system may increase public demand for care and support services.

Most informants believe that the government should play a significant role in providing LTC services to support and complement the care provided by families. The government should supply the medical and nursing component of LTC and also train caregivers, community health nurses, physiotherapists, occupational therapists, social welfare officers, and doctors. The government plays an important role in governance and regulation of formal care providers and in making transport and local environments more accessible to older persons.

Appendix 1 summarizes the discussions with key informants.

B.   Understanding the Supply of Care

1.   Family Care Provision

Currently, home and community-based care services that support aging in place for elders with limitations in ADL and IADL are rare. Often, available residential care services are not appropriate in terms of services or eligibility. The Australian Institute of Health and Welfare defines informal care as "regular and sustained care and assistance provided by a person, such as a family member, friend or neighbor, to the person requiring support." This is the most common form of care in Sri Lanka and other countries.

Informal care at home may be provided by family members. Usually, the primary caregiver is a female relative, resulting from a common belief that "care is the responsibility of the woman." This may account for the low participation of women in Sri Lanka's labor force, which was only 33.6% in 2018 (footnote 17). Among women not in the paid workforce, 61% were engaged in household activities, including caring for children and elders. The economic costs of unpaid family care in Sri Lanka are unknown.[26]

Studies indicate that this type of care is very costly for families. In a study in Canada, a large proportion of respondents felt that caregiving incurs a significant financial strain, with 38% stating that they had to give up other necessities to bear the costs of caregiving for older adults (Lai 2012). The potential negative results of care responsibilities on the financial, physical, and mental well-being of caregivers are well documented in other countries.

The types of care provided by family members include help with ADL and IADL; incontinence care; modifying the home to be more age-friendly; helping older people get medical and nursing care by taking them to the doctor, hospital, or pharmacy; and accompanying the older person to cultural, social, or religious activities. Older people with some functional limitations often contribute to the family (e.g., providing childcare, helping with household chores, or gardening).

Hiring untrained domestic workers is usually less expensive than paying a nursing care provider. Sometimes a domestic worker, who may have been with the family for years, gradually becomes a caregiver as the needs of the elder increase. It is important that they receive information and support and are not exploited.

---

[26]   Asian Development Bank. Key Indicators Database: Sri Lanka. https://kidb.adb.org/kidb/sdbsCountryView/countryViewResult?selectedCountryId=190&selectedCountryShortName= (accessed 9 April 2020).

2.   Trends Influencing Availability of Care

Sri Lanka shifted from extended families to smaller, nuclear families (footnote 3). The average household size decreased from 4.9 people in 1981/1982 to 3.8 in 2016,[27] indicating a decline in the capacity of families to provide required care to older persons.[28]

The dynamics of providing eldercare are influenced by economics and social factors, such as increasing female participation in the labor force and a rise in the internal and external migration of adult children. The number of people leaving the country for foreign employment increased from 42,625 departures in 1990 (0.7% of the labor force) to some 212,162 departures (2.5% of labor force) in 2017.[29] More than 80% of female migrant workers have left Sri Lanka to work as housemaids. Of the total number of migrant workers, more than 50% were unskilled workers (footnote 26). A significant proportion of the labor force is born in districts different from where they are employed. Internal migration for work purposes can affect family relationships: the rate of marriage dissolution among internal migrant women workers was higher compared to nonmigrant women workers.[30]

Compared to 1992, the 2006 World Bank study reported that there had been no major change in the living arrangements of older people. This is not particularly surprising given the social and cultural values of Sri Lankans. Studies show that elders and caregivers alike believe that family members have a duty to provide care for parents and other family elders.[31]

3.   Care Ecosystem: Supporting Services

Health-care services. The Sri Lankan health-care system encompasses several different systems of medicine: Western, Ayurvedic, Unani, Siddha, homeopathic, and acupuncture, of which Western is the most commonly used.[32] A combination of Western and Ayurvedic medicine is provided by both the public and private sectors. The public sector's curative care network includes teaching hospitals with specialized services as well as small dispensaries that provide only outpatient services. Medical Officers of Health Units provide most preventive health services through teams of doctors, community midwives, and others.[33] The private health sector provides curative care and some preventive care at a cost. The National Health Strategic Master Plan 2016–2025 aims to strengthen the primary care network and the shared care cluster model. It is important when planning the LTC system to consider how the system could interface with this new model. Given that Ayurvedic medical care is popular with older people, it will also be important to consult with the new Ayurvedic Medical Council.

More than 1,000 institutions comprise the MOH's integrated network of public health centers. This dense network allows most Sri Lankans to live within 3 kilometers of a facility. Patients can visit any hospital without restriction and referral systems are not enforced. Despite low budgetary spending, studies indicate that the government is able to maintain these facilities because (i) the technical efficiency of its delivery system keeps

---

[27]   Government of Sri Lanka, Department of Census and Statistics. 2018. *Household Income and Expenditure Survey 2016*. Sri Lanka.
[28]   K.D.M.S. Kaluthantiri. 2014. Ageing and the Changing Role of the Family in Sri Lanka. PhD thesis. University of Adelaide.
[29]   Government of Sri Lanka, Bureau of Foreign Employment. 2017. *Annual Statistical Report of Foreign Employment 2017*. Sri Lanka: Research Division, Sri Lanka Bureau of Foreign Employment.
[30]   S. Ukwatte. 2004. Dominance of Females in Internal Migration in Sri Lanka. *Sri Lanka Journal of Population Studies*. 7 (1).
[31]   M. H. Watt, B. Perera, T. Østbye, S. Ranabahu, H. Rajapakse, and J. Maselko. 2014. Caregiving Expectations and Challenges among Elders and Their Adult Children in Southern Sri Lanka. *Ageing and Society*. 34 (5). 838–858. doi: 10.1017/S0144686X12001365.
[32]   Government of Sri Lanka, Medical Statistics Unit. 2014. *Annual Health Bulletin*. Colombo: Ministry of Health, Nutrition and Indigenous Medicine.
[33]   R. Rannan-Eliya and L. Sikurajapathy. 2009. Sri Lanka: "Good Practice" in Expanding Health Care Coverage. *Research Studies Series*. Colombo: Institute for Health Policy.

costs down and, (ii) richer patients are implicitly encouraged to use private clinics so as not to burden the public health system (footnote 30). Regardless of their circumstances, all citizens of Sri Lanka qualify for free health care from state providers.

Compared to younger people, more men and women aged 60+ years use inpatient and outpatient care. Older age groups account for a substantially higher share of health expenditure compared to other age groups. In 2005, the proportion of the population aged 60–74 years was only 8%, but their share of health expenditure was 13%. Moreover, the proportion of the population older than 74 years was only 2%, while their share of expenditure was 4%.[34]

The National Noncommunicable Disease Prevention and Control Program was established in 1999 in response to the rising prevalence of noncommunicable diseases. Under this program, Healthy Lifestyle Centres were established in 2011 to provide screening of noncommunicable diseases. This screening program originally targeted people aged 40–65 years, but advocacy efforts succeeded in forcing the government to remove the upper age limit in 2016. In 2015, 814 Healthy Lifestyle Centres in primary health-care institutions across the country screened 391,044 people (i.e., 6.5% of the target population) (Medical Statistics Unit 2015).

At present, the public sector provides no formal long-term health-care services. However, the National Elderly Health Policy (February 2017) has identified some strategies to introduce and develop comprehensive LTC services (see section III.C.1).

Social services. The Ministry of Social Empowerment and Welfare comprises more than 10 institutions that provide social services, including financial, material, and other social assistance, to older people, persons with disabilities, single-parent households, and low-income families. The NSE is in charge of providing these services to elders (see section III.C.2).

Enabling environments. The Disabled Persons (Accessibility) Regulations, No. 1 (2006) established specifications for public buildings, public spaces, and places that provide common services to ensure that persons with disabilities can adequately access these services.

The NSE issues Elders' Identity Cards to people older than 60 years. This card gives the holders certain privileges (e.g., priority service in government and private sector services, higher interest rates on savings, and discounts on the purchase of medicines). However, the country diagnostic study (CDS) team's focus group discussion revealed that the card is rarely recognized and did not actually bring the elders many benefits. There is a need to raise awareness and respect for the Elders' Identity Card.

The Global Network for Age-Friendly Cities and Communities is an initiative began by WHO to improve enabling environments for older persons. In Sri Lanka, the Wellawaya Division in Uva Province joined the network in 2012 with support from the WHO country office, the Ministry of Social Services, and the MOH. Elders' Committees and Disabled People's Organizations are key stakeholders. This approach aims to create an inclusive environment for older persons and also for people with disabilities. A 10-year plan, began in 2013, offers learning opportunities for other cities and communities across the country.[35]

---

[34]   R. Rannan-Eliya and Associates. 2008. Population Ageing and Health Expenditure: Sri Lanka 2001–2101. In *Research Studies Series 2*. Colombo: Institute for Health Policy.
[35]   World Health Organization. *Age-Friendly World*. Wellawaya, Sri Lanka. https://extranet.who.int/agefriendlyworld/network/wellawaya/ (accessed 8 June 2018).

C.   Regulatory and Policy Framework

1.   Policy Landscape

The Constitution of Sri Lanka grants all citizens the right to health care, while legislation such as the Protection of the Rights of Elders Act (No. 9 of 2000) and the Protection of the Rights of Elders (Amendment) Act, No. 5 of 2011 focus more on elders' rights and welfare. Table 11 presents legislation and policies relating to older persons.

The National Elderly Health Policy of Sri Lanka was launched in February 2017 to reflect the government's commitment to provide comprehensive health-care services to older persons, and the delivery plan mandated the redevelopment of underutilized inpatient health-care facilities into LTC facilities. It also proposed a list of identified health-care facilities that could be improved for this purpose. The action plan suggested requiring special human resources development to staff those facilities.

The level of implementation and effectiveness of these laws are rather limited, likely due to financial and human resource constraints that strongly affect implementation.

Table 11: Regulations and Policies Related to Elders and People with Disabilities in Sri Lanka

Year	Law and/or Policy	Description and/or Features	Level of Implementation
Regulations			
2000	The Protection of the Rights of Elders Act, No. 9 of 2000	• Established the National Council for Elders (NCE) to ensure the promotion and protection of the welfare and rights of older persons and help elders live with self-respect, independence, and dignity. • Simultaneously established the National Secretariat for Elders (NSE) to assist the NCE in discharging its functions. • The NCE is responsible for advising the government on matters relating to elders, organizing activities to inculcate the notion of familial duty in caring for elders, maintaining population statistics relating to elders, etc. • The NCE is empowered to acquire properties; construct buildings; open and maintain bank accounts; borrow money; accept and receive grants, donations, and bequests; issue elders' identity cards; establish Elders' Committees, etc. • The act clearly states that adult children should not purposely neglect their parents and that it is the duty of the children to provide the care that elders need. In the absence of this care, the government will step in to provide the appropriate residential facilities required by disadvantaged elders.	Most functions were implemented, except for introducing a health insurance benefit scheme for elders and maintaining a directory of paid and unpaid job opportunities available to elders.

continued on next page

Table 11 continued

Year	Law and/or Policy	Description and/or Features	Level of Implementation
2011	Protection of the Rights of Elders (Amendment) Act, No. 5 of 2011	• Enacted to revise some sections of the legislation of 2000. • Introduced an identity card for every elder to facilitate the receipt of benefits and concessions available to elders in both public and private sector services. • Appointed conciliation officers. • Disseminated knowledge of gerontology and geriatric medicine among persons involved in providing eldercare. • Revised registration requirements of residential care facilities for elders.	Most functions have been implemented, but inefficiencies remain in activities such as registration and monitoring of residential homes for elders. New regulations are being drafted to address these issues.
2006	The Protection of the Rights of Persons with Disabilities Act, No. 28 of 1996 and the Disabled Persons (Accessibility) Regulations, No. 1 of 2006	• Enacted to address issues faced by persons with disabilities with regard to their rights. Section 36 of the Act defines a person with disability as "any person who, as a result of any deficiency in his physical or mental capabilities, whether congenital or not, is unable by himself to ensure for himself, wholly or partly, the necessities of life." • Established the National Council for Disabled Persons (NCPD), whose function is to promote, advance, and protect the rights of persons with disabilities. • Introduced Disabled Persons (Accessibility) Regulations, No. 1 of 2006, which clearly call for all public buildings, public spaces, and places that provide common services (e.g., transportation services and related facilities) to be made accessible to persons with disabilities within the next 3 years.	Not fully implemented and monitored due to practical problems and other inefficiencies in administrative systems.
Policies			
2006	The National Charter for Senior Citizens	• Adopted by the cabinet of ministers to define the rights and responsibilities of older persons in Sri Lanka. • Ensures that senior citizens do not lose their fundamental human rights and are able to participate in economic activities if they wish to do so. Also specifies the responsibilities of senior citizens toward themselves and society. • Encourages an active economic and social lifestyle for senior citizens, if health and personal circumstances allow.	Not fully implemented.
2006	National Policy for Senior Citizens of Sri Lanka	• Adopted by the cabinet of ministers in 2006 • Aims to support older persons' continued well-being in the latter stages of life, regarding finances, health care, housing, social welfare and other needs, and to provide protection against abuse and exploitation.	Not fully implemented.

continued on next page

Table 11 continued

Year	Law and/or Policy	Description and/or Features	Level of Implementation
		• Recognizes the contributions of nongovernment organizations (NGOs) and the private sector, religious and cultural organizations, and the media as partners in providing care for senior citizens. • Pledges to strengthen human resources and resource allocation for health services that cater especially to older persons (e.g., creating cadres of specialists like geriatricians and community health nurses). The policy also has a strategic plan of action for implementing and monitoring progress. There are 17 strategies altogether. • Neither the policy nor the subsequent strategies or action plans emphasize the need for long-term care (LTC) in old age, although certain action points are relevant to LTC. • The policy and the action plan have led to some important legislative developments (e.g., amendment of the Protection of the Rights of Elders Act in 2011 to introduce elders' identity cards and Elders' Committees).	
2017	National Elderly Health Policy of Sri Lanka 2017	• Reflects the government's commitment to provide comprehensive health-care services to older persons. • Aims to ensure a comprehensive health-care package for older persons to maintain good health; make available health promotion and preventive health services to people of all ages; provide guidance to providers of health care for elders from the private and NGO sectors; equitable delivery of health services to older persons; make available well-trained human resources to manage older people's health care; and empower eldercare societies, volunteers, and the community on all aspects related to the care of older persons. • The delivery plan for the policy proposed (i) repurposing the current Leprosy Hospital in Handala into a National Institute for Geriatric Medicine as a center of excellence for older people's health care; (ii) establishing stroke units at selected hospitals; (iii) improving rehabilitation units in selected hospitals; (iv) improving infrastructure facilities and services to make them elder-friendly; and (v) developing prosthetics and orthotics centers in accordance with national guidelines. • Develop long-term health-care institutions for older people in identified hospitals across the country. • Aims to improve primary care services and facilities that focus on health care for older persons. • Aims to develop and improve human resources to improve cadre numbers for hospitals identified for development as long-term health-care institutions rehabilitation units for older persons.	Launched in February 2017.

continued on next page

Table 11 continued

Year	Law and/or Policy	Description and/or Features	Level of Implementation
2017	New policy for the elderly (draft)	The NSE has drafted a new policy for improving services for older persons, to be submitted to the cabinet for approval. Not yet available publicly, the policy covers certain areas that were not prioritized previously (e.g., improving accessibility for older people with mobility impairments, developing transport systems to make them more elder-friendly, etc.).	Still in drafting stage before submission to the cabinet for approval.

Source: Author.

2. Stakeholder Landscape: Leadership, Governance, and Coordination

The MOH, together with the newly established State Ministry of Primary Health Care, Epidemics and COVID Disease Control, are responsible for policy and formulating LTC services for older persons. The NSE, under the state ministry, is responsible for coordinating the services, with the Youth Elderly Disabled and Displaced unit, MOH. The MOH is responsible for providing medical and nursing services for older persons.

The NSE-provided services for older persons include

- establishing and maintaining day-care centers,
- establishing divisional-level Elders' Committees,
- conducting preretirement seminars,
- issuing intraocular lenses for older cataract patients,
- registering organizations and institutions that provide services for older persons,
- renovating eldercare homes,
- paying the "Wadihiti Saviyata Jeshta Purawasi Deemanawa" allowance to eligible elders,
- issuing identity cards to elders,
- training home care service assistants,
- operating a maintenance board for neglected or poor elders, and
- commemorating International Elders Day.

Currently, LTC service provision and support for family caregivers is insufficient.

Elder rights promotion officers (ERPOs) are divisional secretariat-level officers of the NSE who are responsible for carrying out a long list of duties, including

- arranging for low-income people older than 70 years to receive an allowance under the "Wadihiti Saviyata Jeshta Purawasi Deemanawa" scheme;
- monitoring and coordinating the village, district, and provincial Elders' Committees;
- disseminating NSE publications to the general public;
- making arrangements to issue elders' identity cards to people older than 60 years;
- educating the general public on programs that the provincial councils and Grama Sevaka Offices conduct regarding older people;
- making applications to the maintenance board on behalf of elders who are not supported by their children or are neglected;
- conducting workshops to educate government and nongovernment officials;

- identifying and making arrangements to provide security for destitute elders older than 60 years;
- identifying and registering eldercare homes, providing advice on how to register and how to construct eldercare homes in accordance with the NSE standards;
- educating children and young people on their duties toward elders; and
- conducting and coordinating health clinics for older persons.

The MOH provides general medical and nursing services for all elders, but does not currently provide any services focused solely on LTC. Such services include diagnostic and laboratory services, screening, rehabilitative referrals, and training health-care providers.

At the district level, the staff (i.e., public health midwives, public health inspectors, and public health nursing sisters) at the Medical Officer of Health perform some tasks that provide eldercare, although none of these duties are included in their job description. For example, public health midwives who visit homes to check on new mothers and babies might also check the blood pressure and eyesight of any older people in that household. They are also a source of comfort to older people, who share their problems and news with the public health midwives.

The Office of the Medical Officer of Health also conducts noncommunicable disease clinics in their area, and in addition to health services help identify patients who suffer from any diseases. However, they do not target older people in particular. At the divisional and provincial levels, health service officers have no official duties regarding LTC for older persons, but rather provide the same health services as they do for the general population.

The role of the Ministry of Finance (MOF) in resource allocation is also key to discussing the establishment of an LTC system. The MOF noted the rapidly aging population in 2016: "It is widely recognized that the ageing population will have far reaching implications for the society and for the economy, given the unique challenges that an ageing population will create, including the significant additional demands for more organized aged care systems and the associated financing and delivery of services for elders in need of care."[36] It is important to carefully cost implementation plans and advocate with the MOF for greater resources for LTC.

Coordination mechanisms. The NSE coordinates with the Youth Elderly Disabled and Displaced unit to provide training for in-home care service assistants. The NSE also coordinates with the Ministry of Women's Affairs on a few matters relating to older women, the Ministry of Education on formulating education policies, and the Ministry of Law and Order to establish and maintain a hotline dedicated to older persons. Although the NSE coordinates most activities implemented by different government authorities, there is no higher-level authority to oversee and monitor this coordination mechanism and ensure that all activities related to elders are integrated, rather than simply allocated, with different organizations and have adequate resources.

Civil society, nongovernment organizations, and partnerships. A few NGOs focus on providing eldercare, although very few provide LTC exclusively for elders. The Sarvodaya Suwawetha Movement operates three eldercare homes, while HelpAge Sri Lanka conducts training programs for in-home care assistants and volunteers and provides home care assistance services. Many of these programs are ad hoc and depend on funds available to the NGO. There is potential for the government to fund these services and systematically reach more elders in need of LTC.

---

[36]   Government of Sri Lanka, Ministry of Finance. 2016. *Government Budget Speech 2016.* http://www.treasury.gov.lk/documents/10181/28027/ Budget+Speech+2016/07f592ff-770f-4d71-8c26-b06de595eab0.

Some NGOs have provided support to family caregivers. This is important because family caregivers often work very hard; may have interrupted sleep; may be at risk of back pain from lifting; lack an income and cannot save for their own old age; and may suffer stress, isolation, and anxiety. Their contribution should be included in the national accounts, and they should receive a caregiver allowance. Family caregivers need information, training, access to assistive devices and incontinence aids, supportive counseling, and respite care for their older family member when needed.

There is much potential for developing small and micro businesses to provide community-level services at low cost.[37] This presents an opportunity for younger, fit elders to earn money by providing services to elders who need care. Additionally, businesses and unions must recognize employees' need for flexibility to care for family members.

3.   Development and Future Planning

Currently, Sri Lanka lacks regulations or policies that exclusively address LTC for older persons. Moreover, the importance given to LTC by existing regulations and policies is inadequate to meet the future burden. Therefore, national dialogue must begin with explaining (i) the exact nature of LTC for elders, what it involves, and why it is a problem; (ii) why there will be a growing need for LTC; (iii) why these trends are unavoidable despite cultural considerations; and (iv) what systematic action and policy changes other relevant countries have taken to deal with a similar problem. A wider group of policymakers and the public should understand the need to establish a formal LTC system, formulate policies and regulations, and allot public funding for the system. In the past 7 years alone, numerous consultations have been held on healthy aging, older persons' rights, population health, and population aging. The government has also been involved in regional meetings on LTC and in the Third Review of the Madrid International Plan of Action on Ageing, which covers LTC.

---

[37]   S. Dasanayaka. 2006. Innovative Business Opportunities to Serve Aging Population in Sri Lanka. In S. Sahay, R. Stough, and D. Saradana, eds. *Cases in Business Management*. New Delhi: Allied Publishers. pp. 291–333.

IV. SERVICE PROVISION FOR LONG-TERM CARE

A.   Types of Organizations

Day care and community care. NSE- and NGO-operated day-care centers are places where older persons can engage in productive and social daytime activities with their peers. Day-care centers provide opportunities to socialize, exercise, and participate in religious and recreational activities as well as important community-based social care to those requiring LTC. The NSE supports 662 day-care centers around the country.[38] The NSE also provides each center with financial assistance (up to SLRs25,000) for the purchase of equipment and materials. HelpAge Sri Lanka and other NGOs have also supported day-care centers. Potentially, day-care centers can provide care and support to elders and their family caregivers, although currently they generally aim to provide elders who do not need ADL/IADL support a place to socialize and remain active. This helps improve well-being and prevents the decline of functional ability.

There may be other day-care centers and Elders' Clubs operated by small NGOs and village-level committees, but the time and scope of this CDS did not allow for the compilation of a comprehensive list. In other countries, adult day-care centers are part of core service provisions. They provide care support, facilitate social participation and activities, and allow family caregivers to engage in paid employment or have some respite from caregiving.

An example of community-based care is the home care volunteers program conducted by HelpAge Sri Lanka. "Young-old" people (defined as elders between 60 and 70 years old) identified by the Elders' Committees are encouraged to visit and monitor other elders who live in their area. Volunteers participate in a 5-day residential training program on basic first aid, hygiene, and health care, where they learn to (i) identify vulnerable elders and mental illnesses, and (ii) advocate the rights of the elders. They visit homes and gather information on the living arrangements of the elders. They are linked with the Office of the Medical Officer of Health, to which they can provide information about elders in need of care. They also liaise with HelpAge Sri Lanka if an older person requires an assistive device. The full cost for this program is borne by HelpAge Sri Lanka. It has been operating since the 1990s and trains about 200 volunteers every year. Currently, approximately 2,000 volunteers provide these services in the community.

Additionally, different NGOs and government institutions conduct small-scale training programs for caregivers. HelpAge Sri Lanka also trains in-home care assistants in a program for paid caregivers.

Another example of community-based care is HelpAge Sri Lanka's meals on wheels program in Ratmalana. Former members of the HelpAge Ratmalana Day Care Centre who are no longer mobile or

---

[38]   As reported to the IHP.

able to independently attend to their own needs receive daily meals prepared and delivered by someone from the day-care center.

The Protection of the Rights of Elders (Amendment) Act, No. 5 of 2011 required the establishment of Elders' Committees at the level of the Grama Niladhari Divisions, the smallest administrative division in Sri Lanka, as well as at divisional, district, and provincial levels. Currently, two-thirds of divisions (no.=9,269), 64% of divisions (no.=214), 17 of 25 districts, and 4 of 9 provinces have an Elders' Committee (Ministry of Social Empowerment Welfare and Kandyan Heritage 2017). Elders' Committees aim to empower and advocate the rights and welfare of older persons in the relevant area. The National Council for Elders (NCE) establishes and provides financial assistance (SLRs5,000) to each Elders' Committee. Some Grama Niladhari Divisions have more than one community. Some community-level Elders' Clubs have been established with support from NGOs. They have many benefits (e.g., improving social participation, health promotion, and income-generating activities).[39] Currently, their role and responsibilities in relation to LTC are not defined, but they potentially could help coordinate care and support for elders who need help from younger, more fit elder volunteers, or as an income-generating activity. For example, they might deliver a midday meal to elders who cannot cook for themselves, provide company, assist with physical exercises, or offer foot care for diabetics.

Care provided by nursing care services and in-home care assistant services. The types of services provided by private nursing care and in-home care assistants vary, ranging from simply preparing meals to 24-hour nursing care. An in-home nursing care service provides a trained nurse to care for an elder, while in-home care assistant services provide untrained caregivers. Duties vary according to caregiver qualifications and the fees paid to the service provider. From the 2017 CDS survey of eldercare provider institutions, it is estimated that there are about 25 home nursing care service providers, although the exact number is not known due to gaps in the implementation and monitoring of the formal registration system of such providers and regulation of the industry. These home nursing care services provide 24-hour nursing care to about 900 older clients. The services are usually expensive and not affordable for lower-income families.

Care provided by eldercare homes. Sri Lanka has two main types of residential facilities: those primarily designed to provide housing for older people who lack shelter, and those that aim to provide LTC support and nursing care. In the Sri Lankan context, most facilities fall into the first category and are known as "elders' homes" or "eldercare homes." Even if the primary aim is to provide shelter, some residents have or develop needs for LTC support over time. Sri Lanka currently has around 255 eldercare homes serving approximately 7,100 elder residents, two owned by the central government and three by provincial councils (Table 12). The private sector operates around 20 homes; others are not-for-profit and funded by private donations and some government funding. Not-for-profit eldercare homes are usually operated by faith-based organizations and NGOs. Homes for elders registered under the Department of Social Services increased from 68 in 1987 to 162 in 2003.[40]

Five public eldercare homes house 7% of all elder residents, and 220 private (i.e., not for-profit) eldercare homes house 85% of all elder residents. Out of 7,100 elders living in eldercare homes, 14% need assistance with ADL.

Although only 0.2% of older persons' population lives in an eldercare home, 0.6% of male elders and 0.7% of female elders aged 80 years or older live in such facilities (Figure 6). Most people who live in eldercare homes are over 70 years of age (Figure 6). According to CDS survey estimates, over 50% of elders in eldercare homes live in the Western Province, where 28% of the population of the country resides.

---

39   W. Holmes and J. Joseph. 2011. Social Participation and Healthy Ageing: A Neglected, Significant Protective Factor for Chronic Non Communicable Conditions. *Globalization and Health*. 7:43.
40   Government of Sri Lanka, Department of Social Services. 2006. *Statistics 2006*.

**Table 12: Estimated Number of Eldercare Homes and Residents
by Type, 2017**

Type	Homes (no.)	Residents (no.)	Residents per Home (no.)	Residents Needing Assistance with ADL (%)
Public	5	500	100	26
Private (for profit)	30	500	15	24
Private (not-for-profit)	220	6,100	30	12
Total	255	7,100	30	14

ADL = activities of daily living.
Source: Institute for Health Policy. 2017. Survey of Elder Care Provider Institutions. Colombo.

Only 18% of the homes that responded to the CDS survey accepted elders who need 24-hour nursing care, and 30% accepted elders who need assistance with ADL. Most eldercare homes lack the necessary staff or financial resources to care for elders who need 24-hour nursing care and assistance with ADL. In practice, most residential eldercare homes that provide such assistance do so because they continue to accommodate elders who once were physically able but now need assistance. Most eldercare homes take residents to the nearest government hospital for medical and nursing care.

A few private eldercare homes offer respite care, but there is little information about how this service is used. Figure A4.2 in Appendix 4 presents further information.

Comprehensive data on the health and social profiles of elders who receive services from in-home nursing care services and eldercare homes are not available, but the understanding is that most residents at public and not-for-profit eldercare homes have no family support. In the Sri Lankan context, the primary purpose of eldercare homes is to provide residence to elders who have shelter or family support. No systematic and representative

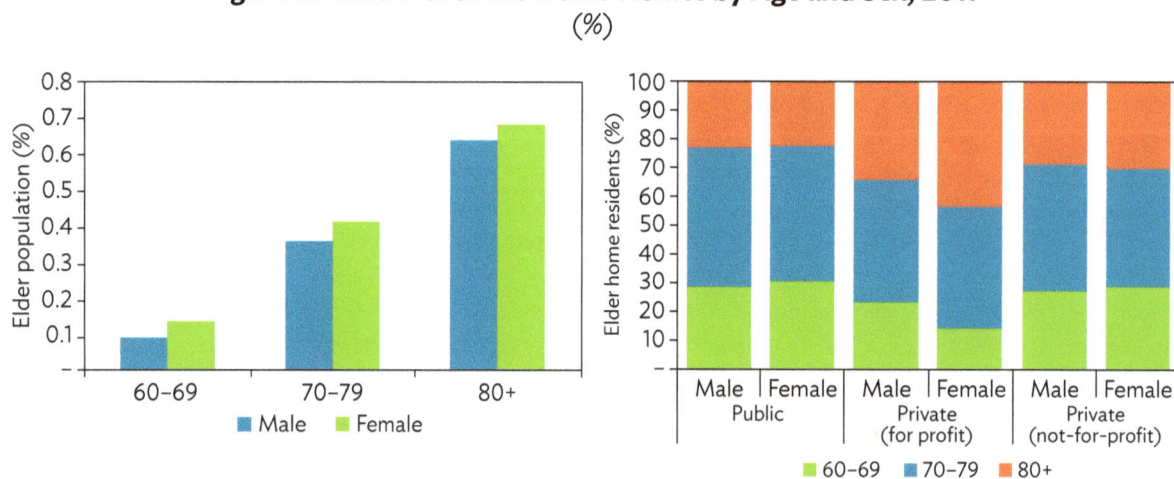

Figure 6: Residents of Eldercare Homes by Age and Sex, 2017
(%)

Source: Institute for Health Policy. 2017. Survey of Elder Care Provider Institutions. Colombo.

study describes the health and social profiles of elders who receive LTC. However, useful qualitative studies have been conducted.[41]

1.   Coordinated and Integrated Care

Delivering person-centered, integrated care requires a coordinated and comprehensive LTC system. Integrated care entails promoting communication and sharing information between service providers, smoothing the path from acute care to transitional care to LTC, and building holistic care services based around the entirety of a person's needs. Integrated care requires (i) participatory care assessment and planning, (ii) named care coordinators, (iii) multidisciplinary teams to develop and implement care plans, (iv) investment in information technology and payment systems that favor care coordination, and (v) patient follow-up. Although Sri Lanka currently lacks this degree of coordination, the National Health Strategic Plan 2016–2025 details the MOH's plan to improve vertical integration within the health system and strengthen the primary care in response to population aging and the related epidemiological shift.[42] A Shared Care Cluster model for primary health care, which could link with LTC efforts, is currently being piloted. Coordination between social welfare and health services at the community level is not integrated, and relevant stakeholders have identified this gap. Moving toward a coordinated LTC system will require careful planning, a greater understanding of LTC, and consideration of a design appropriate to the national context.

2.   Assistive Devices

The consensus is that assistive devices (e.g., wheelchairs) are quite costly, making them unaffordable for many low-income individuals. Government programs and NGOs sometimes provide less costly aids (e.g., eyeglasses and hearing aids), but many elders who need eyeglasses do not have them. A 2003 survey of elders reported that 33% of older population had an unmet need for eyeglasses and 6% had an unmet need for hearing aids (Table 13). Half of those with poor vision use aids to improve their sight, while only 11% use hearing aids out of those who need to use one. Problems with hearing and walking appear to be more prevalent in the rural and estate sectors than in the urban sector (Table 14).

Table 13: Unmet Needs for Equipment and Aids among Older Persons, 2003

Equipment/Aids	Total (%)
Wheelchairs	1.5
Crutches	0.5
Walkers	1.0
Bedpans	1.4
Eyeglasses	33.2
Hearing aids	5.8

Source: National Survey on Elders 2003-2004, National Secretariat for Elders.

---

[41]   M. Gamburd. 2013. Care Work and Property Transfers: Intergenerational Family Obligations in Sri Lanka. *Transitions and Transformations: Cultural Perspectives on Aging and the Life Course*; C. Lynch and J. Danely, eds. *Transitions and Transformations: Cultural Perspectives on Aging and the Life Course*; and K. D. M. S. Kaluthantiri. 2014. Ageing and the Changing Role of the Family in Sri Lanka. PhD thesis. University of Adelaide.

[42]   Government of Sri Lanka, Ministry of Health. *National Health Strategic Plan 2016–2025*. http://www.health.gov.lk/enWeb/HMP2016-2025/ Health%20%20Admin%20-%20%20HRH.pdf.

Between 2006 and 2016, it appears that there was a slight increase in the use of eyeglasses and hearing aids among older persons (Figure 7), but the use of hearing and walking aids is still relatively low and similar between the different sectors. The need to increase the use of hearing aids and walking aids is urgent across all sectors and to increase the use of vision aids in the rural and estate sectors.

Table 14: Use of Disability Aids by Sector, 2006 and 2016
(%)

| | 2006 | | | | 2016 | | | |
| | Sector | | | Total (%) | Sector | | | Total (%) |
	Urban	Rural	Estate		Urban	Rural	Estate	
Elders with disability/difficulty								
Poor vision	67.4	70.4	67.4	69.3	73.0	77.6	50.0	70.3
Hearing problems	24.9	27.8	29.5	27.0	18.4	25.9	22.4	22.2
Walking problems	...	...	...	...	18.9	32.7	40.8	28.7
Elders with disability/difficulty and using an aid								
Poor vision	54.7	48.7	34.5	49.7	79.9	44.4	30.6	57.3
Hearing problems	3.3	2.8	2.6	3.0	13.5	6.7	18.2	11.3
Walking problems	...	...	...	...	32.9	26.7	33.8	30.3

... = data not available.

Sources: Author's calculations based on World Bank. 2006. Sri Lanka Aging Survey; and Government of Sri Lanka, Ministry of Health, Directorate for Youth, Elderly and Disabled Persons. 2016. Report on the institutional survey and community survey in selected areas of Sri Lanka on older people's healthcare.

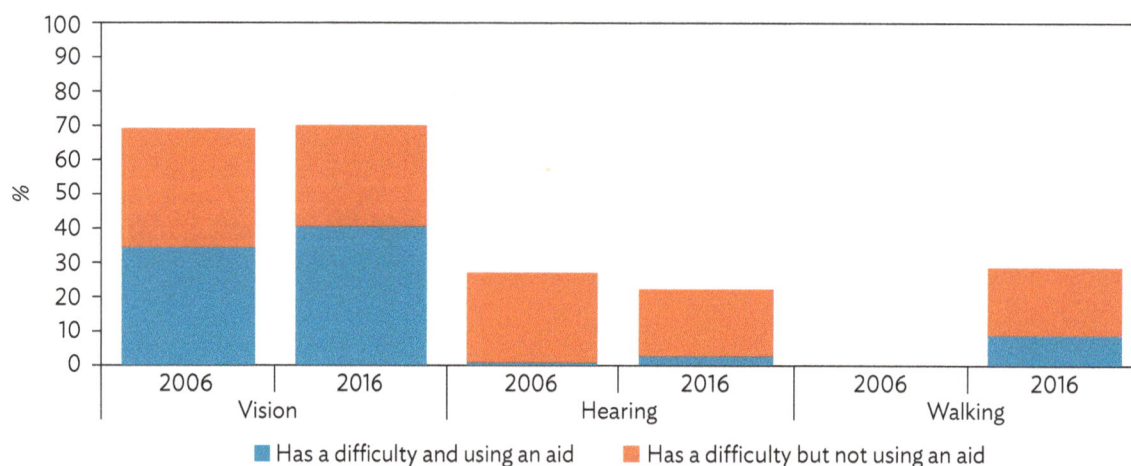

Figure 7: Use of Assistive Devices by Older Persons, 2006 and 2016

Note: Data on difficulties with walking and the use of an aid for walking are not available in Sri Lanka Aging Survey 2006.

Sources: Author's calculations based on World Bank. 2006. Sri Lanka Aging Survey; and Government of Sri Lanka, Ministry of Health, Directorate for Youth, Elderly and Disabled Persons. 2016. Report on the institutional survey and community survey in selected areas of Sri Lanka on older people's healthcare.

B.   Quality Management of Long-Term Care

1.   Existing Quality Management Tools

Registration of eldercare homes and in-home nursing care providers. Under the Protection of the Rights of Elders Act, No. 9 of 2000, any person or organization that provides services or assistance in any form or manner, voluntarily or otherwise, to older persons may register with the NSE. This vague definition was amended in 2011 to say that every person or organization, voluntarily or otherwise, that is engaged in the establishment and maintenance of any institution intended for providing residential care to more than five elders must register with the NSE. The amendment adds that failure to comply with this requirement is an offense.

The Private Medical Institutions (Registration) Act, No. 21 of 2006 and the Extraordinary Gazette No. 1489/18 of 22 March 2007 require nursing care service providers to register with the Private Health Sector Regulatory Council (PHSRC) as a private medical institution. Registration must be done annually through the Provincial Director of Health Services (PDHS). The PHSRC will direct unregistered institutions to register. The PHSRC may shut down any institution that fails to comply with the registration requirement.

Standards of operations for eldercare homes. Protection of the Rights of Elders regulations were in force from 2000 to 2004, then were succeeded in October 2004 by publication of the Standards for Eldercare Homes. The 2004 standards were superseded in 2015 by the Sri Lanka Standard (SLS) 1506:2015 for eldercare homes. Appendix 3 includes important points from that document.

Because the SLS was based on the NSE's 2004 standards, the two documents are similar. An institution must apply with the Sri Lanka Standards Institute (SLSI) to obtain SLS certification. The SLSI conducts regular checks to ensure that the institution continues to maintain the standards.

The registration of eldercare homes was halted in 2015 after practical limitations were encountered in the registration process.[43] It remains uncertain when the new standards will become effective.

Guidelines for the operation of in-home nursing care services. The PHSRC sets guidelines for the operation of in-home nursing care services. The PDHS is required to check that an institution renewing its registration meets the guidelines and is, therefore, responsible for overseeing the quality standards for in-home nursing care institutions.

The guidelines require in-home nursing care institutions to

- employ a full-time qualified nursing officer,
- be overseen by a qualified medical officer,
- show the existence of a mechanism to cover emergencies,
- employ a minimum of 10 caregivers, and
- have an effective communication system that allows them to communicate with their employees.

The guidelines also require employed caregivers to

- possess a certificate from a government-approved training institute and be able to prove their skills and knowledge, and
- carry a basic tool kit necessary for minimum patient care.

---

[43]   As reported to the IHP.

2.   Existing Structures

Although many eldercare homes are registered with the NSE in accordance with the 2011 legislation, others are unregistered. Elder rights promotion officers (ERPOs) are required to register any homes they encounter, provide advice on how to register, and monitor these institutions.

However, registration was halted in 2015 to develop and approve a new process, which will require eldercare homes to maintain standards consistent with SLS 1506:2015. This process is currently pending approval by the NCE and the cabinet.

The PHSRC requires submission of applications and other documents for registration of in-home nursing care services to the NCE through the PDHS office. After checking the institution for eligibility and compliance with standards, the PDHS forwards its recommendation to the NCE. Institutions that do not qualify for accreditation will get time to address shortcomings and meet standards.

3.   Areas for Future Development

Interventions that might influence quality of care include legal registration of eldercare homes (administered by the NSE) and legal registration of in-home nursing care services (administered by the PHSRC). Priorities for future development should include strengthening the registration process, developing quality standards, and strengthening the monitoring process.

Developing a skilled workforce to provide LTC services for older persons is of paramount importance. The government should develop standards, curricula, and accreditation of qualifications, and encourage both public and private training institutes to introduce required training courses.

Constructing new infrastructure and renovating existing infrastructure in care-providing institutions according to established standards and careful monitoring also need attention.

C.   Human Resources and Long-Term Care

1.   Who Provides Care?

Family caregivers and domestic workers provide most care of older persons. Trained in-home care assistants receive training in some LTC services. Further, doctors, nurses, social workers, physiotherapists, occupational therapists, and others sometimes provide LTC services to older persons.

It is not possible to provide the number, age, and gender profiles of LTC workers since none of the cadres are dedicated to LTC alone. Table 15 presents the qualifications and tasks of health workers, social workers, and others who provide LTC services to older persons.

Volunteers. Elders' Committees and NGOs usually operate volunteer networks. Volunteers provide support with IADL (e.g., preparing meals, shopping for groceries, or spending time with older people), but usually do not provide personal care.

HelpAge Sri Lanka's home care volunteer program is an effective model for implementing a network of voluntary caregivers, whereby able elders can be mobilized to provide community-based care by trained volunteers at the village level. It has proved valuable in rural areas with strong community ties.

In-home care assistants. Legally, in-home care assistants do not require training. However, most agencies provide some kind of training or recruit trained people. Such training varies greatly because Sri Lanka has no standard curriculum or standardized qualification.

Elder rights promotion officers and social workers. ERPOs must hold a bachelor degree. Currently, 100 ERPOs deliver services coordinated by the NSE, at a ratio of about 1:25,000 older people or more. Although this limits the role they can play at an individual level, they can coordinate the work of social welfare officers who provide social protection to older persons. ERPOs are not evenly distributed around the country, raising concerns about equity of service provision.

Social service officers (i.e., social workers employed by the State Ministry of Primary Health Care, Epidemics and COVID Disease Control) work at the community level, but official duties focus on domains such as poverty and children. Expanding their scope to include elder issues is unlikely, due to the workload in the current scope of their work.

Table 15: Summary of Human Resources Engaged in Providing Long-Term Care for Older Persons

Role	Tasks	Qualifications and Training
Family, friends, or neighbors	Informal care and/or primary caregivers	No training
Nurses from nursing care services and eldercare homes	• ADL • Some IADL, but not for services such as cooking, personal care, nursing care, assistance in obtaining medical care	• 3-year diploma in nursing, bachelor degree in nursing, or other private training, • PHSRC training
Home care assistants	• ADL • IADL • Personal care • Some nursing care • Assistance in obtaining medical care	• Some have 1–3 weeks training • Some have no training
Volunteers	Social care	Some have 3–5 days training
Medical officers	Diagnosis and management of medical conditions	• Full-time, 5-year medical degree (including 1-year mandatory clinical training) • Postgraduate diploma in eldercare • MD in geriatric medicine • Optional training programs in geriatric medicine (not certified)
Physiotherapists	Diagnosis of physical rehabilitation needs and management of rehabilitation conditions	• 2-year diploma or bachelor degree in physiotherapy • 3-year diploma in orthotics and prosthetics
Occupational therapists	Diagnosis and management of occupational needs	2-year diploma
Speech therapists	Diagnosis and management of speech disorders	BS in speech and hearing science
Elder rights promotion officer	• Case management • Monitoring eldercare provider institutions	• Bachelor degree approved by University Grants Commission • Possible additional diploma in gerontology

ADL = activities of daily living, BS = Bachelor of Science, IADL = instrumental activities of daily living, MD = medical doctor, PHSRC = Private Health Sector Regulation Council.

Source: Author.

Nurses. Currently, Sri Lanka's 17 national nurse-training schools produce roughly 2,500 nurses per year. The diploma in nursing is awarded at the end of a 3-year training period. A bachelor of science (BS) degree in nursing also provides entry into the service at a higher level (i.e., Sister). Armed with either qualification, a person can register with the Sri Lanka Medical Council to become a registered nurse. A nurse must be registered to serve in a government medical institution. In 2015, Sri Lanka had 202 nurses per 100,000 people (Sri Lanka Essential Health Package 2019).

Some nursing courses now include community health nursing and geriatric nursing. Nurses training at the Kotelawa Defence University Faculty of Allied Health Services can include a comprehensive Community Health Nursing module in its curriculum. Despite some small community health nursing projects, larger-scale implementation has not happened due to the great shortage of nurses in hospitals.

Many private institutes provide nurses training (but not a bachelor degree) that qualifies graduates to serve only in private medical institutions. The PHSRC provides some training to improve the quality of such nurses.

Medical officers (doctor). To practice medicine in Sri Lanka, an individual is required to possess a bachelor of medicine, bachelor of surgery (MBBS) or medical doctor (MD) degree as well as registration by the Sri Lanka Medical Council, and must also demonstrate competency in clinical procedures in the capacity of medical officer. Currently, eight state universities and a lateral entry format for graduates from foreign universities produce about 1,500 medical interns biannually. Upon completing a 1-year internship, graduates are entitled to practice medicine by themselves.

Figure 8: Medical Officers and Nurses per 1,000 People in Sri Lanka and Selected Countries, 2010–2014

(no.)

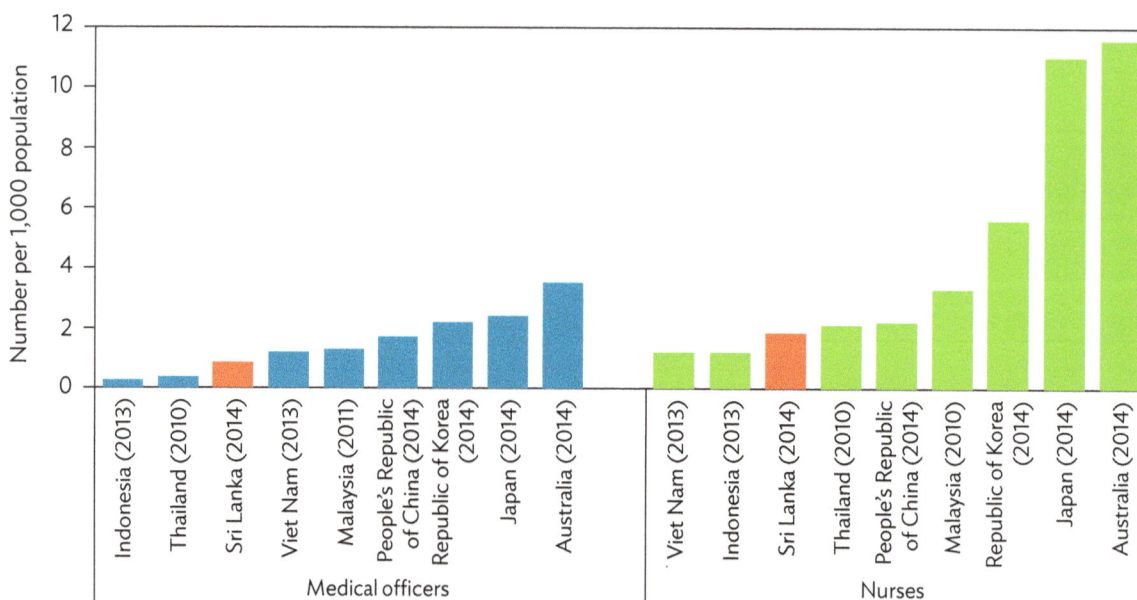

Sources: OECD/WHO. 2016. *Health at a Glance: Asia/Pacific 2016: Measuring Progress towards Universal Health Coverage*; and Government of Sri Lanka, Medical Statistics Unit. 2014. *Annual Health Bulletin*. Colombo: Ministry of Health, Nutrition and Indigenous Medicine.

Sri Lanka currently has 87 medical officers per 100,000 people (Sri Lanka Essential Health Package 2019). The current cadre of medical officers can provide care to elders. Since there is strong interest in this field, it is possible to establish a cadre of doctors who specialize in geriatric medicine and care of older persons. Figure 8 compares the number of medical officers and nurses per 1,000 people in Sri Lanka with other selected countries in Asia and the Pacific.

Around 150 doctors provide medical care, mostly on a visiting basis, and 1,500 caregivers (including nurses, volunteers, trained and untrained attendants) provide care in eldercare homes (Table 16). Each eldercare home has about five residents per caregiver and around 40 physiotherapists.

Table 16: Estimated Number of Medical and Caregiver Staff Employed by Eldercare Homes, 2017

Staff Type	Total (%)
Doctors	150
Nurses	200
Trained attendants	400
Untrained attendants	500
Volunteers	450
Physiotherapists	40

Source: Institute for Health Policy. 2017. Survey of Elder Care Provider Institutions. Colombo.

An estimated 100 nurses, 800 trained attendants, and 500 untrained attendants work for in-home nursing care services, caring for older persons and other people who need LTC. However, families may hire caregivers from in-home nursing care services, home care assistant services, or through other family connections. No data are available regarding the total number of trained and untrained caregivers who provide LTC for older persons.

2.   Caregiver Workforce

The IHP Survey of eldercare providers estimates the monthly income of a caregiver hired from an in-home nursing care provider institution at SLRs30,000–SLRs72,000 ($200–$480). A caregiver's daily rate depends on the services provided, the training of the caregiver, and the in-home nursing care provider institute they are hired from.

3.   Workforce Management

Currently, Sri Lanka has no national standard for evaluating care performance, career structure, and incentives that focus on LTC. Different professions and institutions use their own systems and methods to evaluate performance.

4.   Responsibilities for Developing the Workforce

No agency is formally responsible for developing an LTC workforce in Sri Lanka. However, the Postgraduate Institute of Medicine (PGIM), the NSE, the MOH, and the Sri Lanka Association of Geriatric Medicine (SLAGM) have taken the initiative in developing some of the eldercare workforce.

The PGIM grants eligible persons a postgraduate diploma in medicine for older people. The course includes theoretical and clinical components. The theoretical component consists of training in geriatric medicine and/or surgery, evidence-based practices, preventive medicine and health promotion, ethical and legal issues, cancer care and palliative care, clinical nutrition management, rehabilitation, and spiritual health (PGIM 2013). The clinical component includes training in general medicine, surgery, psychiatry, and neurology (PGIM 2013). The PGIM plans to commence a doctorate in medicine and board certification in geriatric medicine soon. PGIM programs are optional qualifications for medical officers.

The SLAGM was established in 2014 by a group of doctors who had a strong interest in geriatric medicine. The SLAGM organizes lectures for qualified doctors to promote the understanding of eldercare and geriatric medicine in Sri Lanka. In collaboration with the College of Physicians and the College of General Practitioners, the SLAGM hosts annual symposia to disseminate information on developments in geriatrics and other branches of medicine. It also conducts regional training programs for doctors, nurses, and physiotherapists. Interest in these lectures and training programs is very high among doctors, nurses, students, and other caregivers. The SLAGM also conducts regional health clinics for older persons on an ad hoc basis.

In 2006, the NSE initiated a 3-week training program for home care assistants on how to provide care for older patients. In 2015, the program was developed into a National Vocational Qualification (NVQ) Level 2 qualification, which was conducted and appraised by the National Apprentice and Industrial Training Authority (NAITA). This NVQ 2 qualification was conducted jointly with the NSE and the Directorate for Youth, Elderly and Disabled Persons, Ministry of Health (YED MOH). Instruction was provided free of charge. The NAITA and NSE advertised the course and selected people for the training. The YED MOH provided the curriculum and instructors, particularly regarding health education. The program included 2 weeks of practical training in the National Hospital of Sri Lanka.

Since this NVQ 2 level program began, it has trained about 20–25 people in each batch of students. Because trainees are women, there is a need to increase the male cadre. Upon completion, the trainee receives an NVQ 2 level certificate and is also listed on the NSE's database of trained home care assistants. Currently, the NSE has about 100 trained home care assistants in its database.

The NVQ 2 level qualification was introduced under the One Million Jobs program, and was identified as a way to improve women's participation in the labor force and reduce female worker migration. However, low visibility is a major problem for this program. Newspaper advertisements have not been successful in attracting people into the vocation. To counter this, the NSE plans to initiate a sticker campaign to increase visibility and attempt to reach their target audience. Trained caregivers can earn SLRs30,000–SLRs40,000 ($200–$250) per month, and the NSE reports that the trained caregivers find employment. Retaining trained workers has also been a challenge.

Some NGOs also conduct this sort of training program, but with no formal curriculum or standards. It would be good to amalgamate these different programs and introduce a standard curriculum and qualification at the national level. At present, there is no way to continuously assess caregivers' performance and career development.

The National Institute for Social Development offers a free 18-month part-time diploma course on gerontology and/or eldercare. The NSE facilitates this qualification for its ERPOs. In 2015, 37 ERPOs completed this training, which covers subjects such as social gerontology, aging society and culture, basic research methods, health and aging, Ayurvedic health and eldercare, mental health and counseling, and case management and eldercare.

It is possible to expand the role ERPOs play in providing social care for older people who require LTC. In particular, a case management system could be set up where each officer

- identifies any older people who suffer from major physical and mental conditions and require LTC services, and the kind of care they are receiving (if any) and from whom;
- identifies why a person does not receive adequate care;
- identifies the kind of LTC service required (e.g., income security or a primary caregiver);
- mobilizes resources to provide the care that a person requires, using established volunteer networks and trained caregivers;
- follows up on the case to ensure that the person receives the required care; and
- follows up on all identified people to ensure that their standard of living is maintained.

ERPOs will need LTC training to conduct these tasks. The number of ERPOs would also need to increase significantly to expand the coverage of their services.

D. Financing

1. Economic Background

Sri Lanka is a lower-middle-income country. Its per capita income was $4,102 in 2018, when the country's economy increased by 3.2%. Services contributed 62.0% of GDP, followed by industry (29.4%) and agriculture, forestry, and fishing (8.6%). In 2015–2018, government expenditure was around 20% of GDP (Table 17).

Table 17: Economic Indicators of Sri Lanka, 2015–2018

Indicator	2015	2016	2017	2018
Real GDP ($ billion)	67.4	73.8	82.6	88.9
Real GDP per capita ($)	3,844	2,886	4,105	4,102
Real government expenditure ($ billion)	14.0	14.4	15.8	...
Government expenditure (% of GDP)	20.9	19.5	19.1	18.7
Real government expenditure on social protection and health ($ billion)	2.8	2.7	2.9	...
Government expenditure on social protection and health (% of GDP)	4.2	3.7	3.5	...

... = data not available, GDP = gross domestic product.
Note: Calculated at SLRe1 = $0.0062 based on Asian Development Bank. 2019. *Key Indicators for Asia and the Pacific 2019: Sri Lanka*.
Sources: World Bank. World Development Indicators; and Asian Development Bank. Key Indicators.

Social protection expenditure estimates are from IHP analysis of Sri Lankan social protection schemes in the context of social protection floor objectives (ILO 2016).

2. Funding Sources for Long-Term Care

At present, family members who need LTC for their elders pay for these services themselves. Unfortunately, data on out-of-pocket expenditure for LTC at the household level are not currently available.

Sri Lanka has no systematic data on financial flows to LTC. The Sri Lanka Health Accounts (SLHA) compiled by the IHP do not track LTC expenditure. The IHP is improving its SLHA estimates to track LTC as part of this CDS. SLHA estimates comply with the new version of the international standard—System of Health Accounts

(SHA) 2011—and the first international standard, SHA 1.0. SLHA estimates of current health expenditure will include some LTC spending bundled in existing health services, such as LTC provided by acute-care hospitals, but generally will not include spending solely on LTC outside the MOH.

3.   Financial Management

Health care in Sri Lanka is provided by the government, the private sector, and to some extent, the nonprofit sector. Public sector health care aims to be universally accessible and is free at the point of delivery. Many elders face barriers in accessing health care, presenting challenges to achieving universal accessibility. Barriers include the need to pay for medicines and supplies, and equitable coverage of national health and social services. General revenue taxation finances the government health sector, whereas out-of-pocket spending, personal and enterprise-subsidized insurance, enterprise direct payments, and contributions from nonprofit organizations finance the private health sector.

Health spending was 3.8% of GDP in 2017, of which 1.6% was accounted for by public health expenditure and 2.2% by other financing.[44] The government finances most social services, while nonprofit sector and private donation financing is limited. NGOs and charities are financed by international NGOs, donors, private donations from the general public, and private corporations.

Families currently bear most LTC costs. Services provided by family members are considered unpaid household production. Residential care homes are financed by the nonprofit sector and fees are paid by the resident or covered by charitable donations. In-home nursing care services are financed by out-of-pocket payments.

4.   Costs and Affordability of Formal Care

Rathnayake and Siop (2015) state that low income is a significant determinant of the quality of life of older people. Poverty is linked to health inequalities, and older persons are more vulnerable to the consequences of low income (Rathnayake and Siop 2015). Importantly, a country that lacks a universal social security scheme for elders must pay attention to the availability and affordability of LTC services.

Five schemes pay a monthly pension to eligible members. In 2015, the government spent SLRs154 million on pension payments for these schemes (i.e., 9% of total government expenditure). However, these schemes only cover about 39% of the population older than 60 years. Average monthly pensions per pensioner have fallen since 2012, due to the introduction of a small pension paid to a large number of low-income elders in 2013 (Table 18).

Table 18: Average Monthly Pensions, 2012–2015

Amount	2012	2013	2014	2015
Average monthly pension per pensioner (SLRs)	20,210	18,744	15,563	13,382
Average monthly pension per pensioner ($)	158	145	119	98

Sources: Author calculations based on data provided to the IHP from the Department of Pensions, the Agricultural and Agrarian Insurance Board, and the Social Security Board of Sri Lanka.

---

[44]   World Health Organization. Global Health Expenditure Database. https://apps.who.int/nha/database (accessed 8 April 2020).

Average monthly expenditure per resident was SLRs4,300 ($30) in public eldercare homes and SLRs7,000 ($45) in private (not-for-profit) homes in 2016 (Table 19). Public eldercare homes are predominantly financed by public funds and very limited private donations (2% of expenditure), while 70% of expenditures at private (not-for-profit) eldercare homes are financed by individual donations and not-for-profit organizations. In 2016, the average monthly revenue per elder (i.e., monthly fee paid by the resident) in a private (for profit) eldercare home was SLRs24,000 ($170), which included the cost of services (Table 19). Monthly expenditure for a caregiver hired from an in-home nursing care provider ranges from SLRs30,000 to SLRs72,000 ($200–$480). A considerable gap between the income levels of elders and the current costs of formal care makes formal care unaffordable to most elders.

Table 19: Estimated Expenditure/Revenue at Eldercare Homes by Type of Facility, 2016

Type	Total Expenditure/Revenue		Average Monthly Expenditure/ Revenue per Resident	
	SLRs million	$ million	SLRs	$
Public	30	0.2	4,300	30
Private (for profit)	150	1.0	24,000	170
Private (not-for-profit)	500	3.4	7,000	45

Source: Institute for Health Policy. 2017. Survey of Elder Care Provider Institutions. Colombo.

5. Financial Modeling of Future Needs and Funding, Current Discussions, and Reform Options

The CDS team developed a model to project national health expenditure (Rannan-Eliya and Associates 2008), but it is not currently possible to develop accurate projections of future LTC spending because there is no reliable estimate of current spending or key cost drivers (e.g., the rate at which ADL/IADL dependency changes in different age groups). However, the team developed a tentative projection. Population projections were estimates based on moderate fertility rates from long-term population projections for Sri Lanka 2015–2115 by Abeykoon and de Silva (2016). The need for ADL and IADL assistance was estimated based on data from the World Bank 2006 Sri Lanka Aging Survey and the IHP's eldercare provider institutions database (2017). The team assumed that current levels of need for ADL and IADL would remain unchanged for the next 20 years.

In Sri Lanka, affordable LTC services are not common and therefore are rarely utilized. Therefore, estimating future demand for paid care assuming current demand levels will not provide meaningful information for future planning. Given declining co-residency, increasing levels of female participation in the labor force, and internal and external migration, demand for paid care likely will increase in the future. An equitable system would provide an allowance to family caregivers. Currently, there are no data to estimate the growth in demand for paid care. Data on the total number of people who definitely need care (e.g., the bedridden and severely demented) are also not available. Moreover, the total number of people receiving paid and unpaid care cannot be estimated due to the lack of data on the number of people receiving informal care. Table 20 presents the projected need for care estimates based on the World Bank 2006 Sri Lanka Aging Survey.

Table 20: Future Projections for Need and Demand for Care, 2017–2037

Age (years)	2017		2022		2027		2037	
	Male	Female	Male	Female	Male	Female	Male	Female
Elders who need ADL/IADL assistance								
60–69	134,787	212,368	158,376	244,838	174,954	267,171	195,537	289,952
70–79	99,438	214,184	136,809	292,888	180,240	379,425	237,388	483,152
80+	85,505	154,160	98,900	185,979	125,962	239,187	228,132	423,255

ADL = activities of daily living, IADL = instrumental activities of daily living.

Sources: Author's calculations based on long-term population projections for Sri Lanka 2015-2115 by A.T.P.L. Abeykoon and I. de Silva. 2016. (unpublished); World Bank. 2006. Sri Lanka Aging Survey; and Institute for Health Policy. 2017. Survey of Elder Care Provider Institutions. Colombo.

Current debates on financing long-term care. Although champions of the need to respond to population aging have made some progress within the government, more discussion is necessary among LTC policymakers and financing. Most key informants believe that the government should initiate a formal LTC system for elders who use public financing. Informants acknowledged that LTC is currently not a priority in Sri Lanka, and they believe it will be difficult to allocate public financing for an LTC system considering the country's present economic status and priorities. It is important that public financing for an LTC system is seen as an investment.

Lower-cost options for residential care for older persons should be explored and discussed. This could include the concept of small group homes for four or five elder residents at Grama Niladhari Division level, so that elders could age in place—if not in their own home, at least in their own familiar communities.

Sri Lanka appears to be facing the same demographic challenges that prompted other countries in the region to establish an LTC system supported by public financing. Some countries (e.g., Japan and the Republic of Korea) use social insurance to finance LTC. Other economies such as Hong Kong, China rely primarily on general revenue taxation and direct public delivery of many social services. The transferability of Japanese and Korean reforms to Sri Lanka will be limited because Sri Lanka's health and welfare system relies on financing from general revenue taxation, not social health insurance; thus, the country lacks relevant technical expertise, administrative capabilities and experience, and governance institutions. Yet, the experience of the general revenue taxation-subsidized LTC system in Hong Kong, China's system indicates that even this is not a long-term, sustainable mechanism of care unless Hong Kong, China is willing to increase its financial contribution (Box 2). It would also be useful to look at other countries with a funding legacy similar to Sri Lanka (e.g., Singapore, Australia, and New Zealand) to find potentially relevant experiences.

Box 2: Hong Kong, China's Approach to Health and Welfare Services

Hong Kong, China's approach to health and welfare services relies primarily on general revenue taxation for public financing and utilizes direct government delivery for many social services, whereas private, mostly out-of-pocket, financing pays for private services to fill the shortfalls in government financing and provision. Compared to Japan or the Republic of Korea, this approach is more comparable to that of Sri Lanka. In 1997, Hong Kong, China introduced a government long-term care (LTC) policy in response to its rapid population aging.[a] The policy promotes aging-in-place and subsidized LTC services as an alternative for elders aged 65 years and older through the Social Welfare Department. Community-care and residential-care services are subsidized by the government. Eligibility to receive subsidized services is based on a needs assessment, using a standardized care needs assessment mechanism. If there is no space in care centers, eligible elders are added to a waiting list and accommodated on a first-come, first-served basis.

Community-care services include day-care centers and/or units, a day-respite service for elders, enhanced home- and community-care services, integrated home care services, and home-help services. Day-care centers and/or units provide personal care, nursing care, rehabilitation exercise, meal services, respite services, social and recreational services, etc. Enhanced home- and community-care services and integrated home care services offer personal care, care management, rehabilitation exercise, escort services, etc. Residential care services are for elders aged 65 years or older who cannot receive adequate care at home. People aged 60–64 years may apply if there is a proven need.

The Social Welfare Department introduced a Community Care Service Voucher for the Elderly in September 2013 as a pilot project, which is still in effect and covers 18 districts. Elders on the waiting list for community- or residential-care services are eligible for this voucher. Elders with a voucher can choose community-care services that suit their needs.[b]

In 2013/2014, LTC (health) expenditure in Hong Kong, China was 0.25% of gross domestic product (GDP), with 0.20% of GDP covered by public financing and all expenditure covered by general revenue taxation.[c]

Efforts made by the government to address the LTC needs of its population have been inadequate to meet the growing demand for subsidized LTC services. Demand is rising, resulting in longer wait lists and wait times. In 2014, wait times for subsidized residential-care services were 32–36 months (footnote a). Although the government has increased the number of residential-care facilities over the years, it has not satisfied the demand. The efficiency of the assessment mechanism to screen eligible elders for subsidiary services has declined due to staff shortages. Notably, the effective use of existing residential services is important to reducing the tension between increasing demand and slow expansion of care services (footnote a). In Hong Kong, China, the limited amount of general revenue taxation allocated to LTC (0.2% versus 0.9% of GDP in Japan) appears to be the main constraint preventing the expansion of LTC, and most older persons cannot fall back on private financing.

Sources:
[a] Government of the Hong Kong Special Administrative Region of the People's Republic of China, Audit Commission. 2014. Provision of Long-Term Care for the Elderly. https://www.aud.gov.hk/pdf_e/e63ch01.pdf.

[b] Government of the Hong Kong Special Administrative Region of the People's Republic of China, Social Welfare Department. 2017. Second Phase of the Pilot Scheme on Community Care Service Voucher for the Elderly (Pilot Scheme) https://www.swd.gov.hk/en/index/site_pubsvc/page_elderly/sub_csselderly/id_psccsv/.

[c] Government of the Hong Kong Special Administrative Region of the People's Republic of China, Food and Health Bureau. 2017. Statistics. https://www.fhb.gov.hk/statistics/en/dha/dha_summary_report.htm#A.

V. DISCUSSION AND COMMENTARY

A. Limitations of Findings and Major Knowledge Gaps

Some significant data gaps exist. Most services available for LTC are informal in nature; as such, there were severe limitations in collecting data. Relevant research can be difficult to access. A register of research databases could be established at a central secretariat (e.g., the NSE or the new Centre for Ageing at the University of Colombo).

There is also an urgent need for Sri Lanka to conduct a national survey on aging; this has not been done since 2006. This is essential for better understanding the nature of aging and the issues faced by older persons.

The nature and extent of care provided by family members to elders is unknown. Due to a lack of household or community surveys that included questions on the provision of care to elders, it was not possible to gather this information. In addition, no information is available to assess the financial burden placed on families when caring for elders. Similarly, estimations of existing and projected care needs were not possible. However, focus group discussions with health and social officers, older persons, and key informant interviews (KIIs), provided some anecdotal information on the need, demand, and supply of LTC.

The sample framework for the survey of eldercare provider institutions was based on registration lists available from the NSE and PHSRC and complemented by searching the telephone directory and websites. Despite this effort, the actual number of total eldercare providers remains unknown.

LTC still remains a largely understudied topic in Sri Lanka. Although numerous small studies in varied disciplines have been conducted in relation to aging, few focused on or provided information about LTC.

Out-of-pocket expenditure on LTC for elders is unknown, and gathering such information would require a special household survey. In addition, quantitative information about the affordability of assistive devices for elders is not currently available.

The survey of eldercare providers was designed to gather data on the nature of eldercare, but it did not collect any information on the quality of the services. Bridging this gap would require a more thorough and time-intensive field survey.

Information available regarding the number of social admissions of elders to government institutions is very limited because neither the health management information system nor hospitals keep such records. All hospital records regarding morbidity and mortality for social admissions are classified according to disease.

The informal nature of the LTC system did not allow the CDS team to quantify the number of LTC caregivers for older persons. Consequently, the team could not assess the gap between the existing cadre of caregivers and the required cadre.

B. Strength, Weakness, Opportunity, and Threat Analysis of the Long-Term Care System in Sri Lanka

Table 21: Strength, Weakness, Opportunity, and Threat Analysis of the Long-Term Care System

Strengths	Weaknesses
• Relevant legislation • National health policy on elders, which covers some aspects of LTC • Universal public health-care coverage • Existing dedicated national body for elders • Culture of respect for elders • Availability of academic courses for Geriatric and Gerontology specialty • Availability of mental health and noncommunicable-disease focal points covering all regions • Availability of a wide network of ground-level officers from both health and social ministries • Experience with a successful maternal and child health monitoring and an evaluation system that can be adapted and used in an LTC system	• Lack of knowledge among respective government officials on national health policy for elders • Nonavailability of public LTC provider institutions • Lack of provincial and regional responsibility for LTC service provision • Inadequacy of trained human resources • Lack of monitoring and evaluation of eldercare providers • Lack of retirement planning • Lack of coordinated/integrated care in hospitals • Limited rehabilitation services • Absence of a high-level national coordinating mechanism for LTC services
Opportunities	Threats
• National and international NGO and private-sector interest in LTC provision • Employment opportunities in both public and private sectors • Availability of underutilized public health facilities at divisional level • Established Elders' Committees • Religious and cultural values of looking after elders • Available information technology infrastructure, services, and knowledge • Useful NGO projects that could be scaled up	• Lack of public awareness of need for LTC in old age • Lack of public awareness of existing LTC services • Societal resistance toward institutionalized eldercare • Lack of financial resources for LTC services • Rapid aging of population • Increased urbanization • Increasing number of nuclear families • Internal and external migration

LTC = long-term care, NGO = nongovernment organization.
Source: Author.

C.   Current Debate on Long-Term Care Reform

1.   Integrating Health and Long-Term Care

Sri Lanka has no mechanisms for providing integrated and coordinated services. Comprehensive LTC services cannot be accomplished by a single organization; rather, it would require the participation of many organizations. KIIs revealed the necessity of integrating LTC services with the national health system via a multisectoral (i.e., government, the private sector, and NGOs) approach. Due to multiple stakeholders, establishing the system might require placing a high-level coordination mechanism in the office of the President or Prime Minister. The overall objective of this coordinating body would be to develop and maintain a sustainable and formal LTC system to support and complement informal eldercare.

2.   Modes of Care

Currently, most care is provided informally but with very little support. Integrated home- and community-based services need to be developed to enable self-care of elders. Services to strengthen family care and provide personal care and clinical services must ensure quality and appropriate care for those who lack sufficient informal support and/or complex needs. In-home and community care services should include (i) information and training; (ii) assistance with assessing and modifying homes; (iii) nutrition and meal support; (iv) psychosocial support (e.g., peer groups, befriending schemes); (v) respite services; (vi) home care and in-home nursing; (vii) rehabilitation visits; (viii) access to assistive devices; (ix) counseling and mutual support for caregivers; and (x) a caregiver's allowance or other financial assistance. In conjunction with strengthening home- and community-based care services, quality and appropriate residential care will need further development. Currently, there is a significant degree of cultural stigma associated with residential care homes, but this may change with the development of more appropriate styles of residential care (e.g., small group homes) and growing societal awareness.

3.   Financing

Financial resources are a main constraint on establishing and maintaining a formal LTC system for older persons. The government will finance most of the LTC system aided to a lesser extent by the private and not-for-profit sectors.

VI. CONCLUSION AND POLICY IMPLICATIONS

A.   Gaps in the Long-Term Care System

This CDS illustrates a lack of understanding among society and policymakers on what LTC is and the need for an LTC system for older persons.

Although well informed, officials interviewed for this survey are at an early stage of identifying and understanding the problem of LTC for older persons. Local languages (i.e., Sinhala and Tamil) in Sri Lanka have no commonly understood term for LTC.

Existing laws place the responsibility for eldercare in the hands of adult children, and institutionalized care is stigmatized. The lack of LTC for the more complex needs of older persons is an emerging problem. Steps must be taken to raise awareness among policymakers and the public about the need for LTC in old age and for establishing a formal LTC system for older persons.

A significant gap in providing care is the lack of any public LTC services, whether home-based, community-based, or institutional. Available private LTC services are expensive and not everyone can afford them. Although some eldercare homes provide LTC services, most do not accept elders who require LTC due to lack of resources and facilities. No law prohibits such homes from denying patients on this basis. These issues in the supply of LTC services will need to be addressed by strengthening the capacity for LTC provision.

The National Health Policy on Elders provides only a partial basis for improving LTC health services. Quick and efficient implementation of an LTC policy will support the development and improvement of other aspects of a formal LTC system. An LTC policy must empower provincial and regional officials by defining their roles and responsibilities and by providing the necessary financial and human resources. The LTC system will require an efficient, high-level authority to coordinate all stakeholders.

The main challenge in establishing a formal LTC system will involve overcoming the current inadequacy of trained human resources by

- calculating the required number of health and social-service personnel and other caregivers;
- reviewing the job, responsibilities, and workload of existing cadres to assess the feasibility of expanding their job descriptions to accommodate LTC activities;
- identifying new cadres;
- attracting young people to the newly established jobs through proper training, attractive skills development, career development, and salaries; and
- developing a monitoring and evaluation framework and an LTC information system.

Additionally, existing LTC service providers must undergo proper monitoring and evaluation process. The registration process for service providers will require improvement and quick implementation. This would require formalizing the process, designating an oversight body, and assigning staff to handle the monitoring and evaluation process.

This CDS recommends a strong and integrated national response to raise social awareness of the need for LTC for older persons. Moreover, social awareness must also be raised regarding the need to establish a formal LTC system and support family care for dependent elders.

At the same time, these and other national policies do not address realistic financing for expanded LTC services or the inevitable need for public finance. Without serious consideration of the financial demands and how to resolve them, almost all current policies and government interventions will fail to have significant impact on the problem. Addressing the financial challenges of expanding LTC services should precede the development of more ambitious policies on provision and regulations. Civil society, policymakers, and the public must consider financing LTC expansion as well as the respective roles of individuals, families, and the government in bearing the costs.

B.   Financial Options

Global experience shows other countries depend on public government tax revenues or social insurance contributions to finance health care and social services. Even countries that rely on social insurance mechanisms need substantial public financing from general revenue taxation to support LTC. This study determined that expanding formal LTC for older persons will require government financing.

Considering that existing government service commitments in health care, education, and other social sectors are underfunded, the financing capacity of current government must be reviewed. Because the public lacks awareness of the financial challenge Sri Lanka will face, LTC implementation will be slow until the government increases taxes from the current low level (less than 16% of GDP).

Uncoordinated, ad hoc development of LTC by different ministries could waste limited resources and disrupt the potential for developing a well-designed system. On the other hand, some countries have developed a holistic LTC system through trial and error, including piloting models that lead to the recognition that a strong financing stimulus is required. Therefore, this study recommends a carefully considered and well-planned process to establish a public LTC system, including both financing and delivery components and in parallel with wider government efforts to expand the country's tax base. In the short and medium term, government and researchers could work with other stakeholders to raise awareness of the need for (i) a public LTC system to support older persons and their families, (ii) money to finance such a system, and (iii) gathering data for the planning process. An in-depth study to review the financial options for investments by public–private partnerships could complement efforts to initiate an LTC system.

C.   Action Scenarios

The CDS team's findings and understanding of the country context suggest that Sri Lanka needs a strong, integrated national effort to establish a formal LTC system for older persons. The government should initiate policies and regulations, allocate sufficient public funds, and, ultimately, raise taxes to finance this project. This national effort should involve different government ministries and institutions as well as the private (for-profit and not-for-profit) sectors. It might be necessary to establish a high-level coordination mechanism in the office of the President or Prime Minister to manage all of these stakeholders. The overall objective would be to develop and maintain a sustainable, formal LTC system.

To fully understand the issues and problems regarding LTC for older persons and how underlying needs will change in the future, Sri Lanka urgently needs to conduct a national needs assessment. This process should include collecting more systematic data on the prevalence of physical and mental dependency among older persons and understanding how such data translate into unmet needs for LTC.

Learning from other countries, Sri Lanka could pilot two or three delivery and payment models in different districts to assess the feasibility of adopting and establishing an LTC system that meets the needs of older persons. However, pilot schemes often presuppose that effective policies are put in place to finance the different models.

It is also important to focus on retirement planning, prevention of noncommunicable diseases, and other socioeconomic aspects that could help reduce any future burden on older persons.

D. Strengthening Learning and Dialogue on Long-Term Care

This study prioritized building awareness and understanding the following questions:

- What LTC is, what does it involve, and why is it a problem?
- Why there is a growing need for LTC in Sri Lanka, and why will it require public financing?
- What systematic action and policy changes have other relevant countries taken to deal with a similar problem?

Policymakers and the general public must accept that it is a substantial problem for government and society to initiate an effective dialogue and discuss future policy development. It is vital that policymakers understand the need for substantial public financing to establish an LTC system. European countries spend an average 1.4% of GDP on their LTC systems.

E. Gender and Poverty Analysis

Older women and men have different needs and make different contributions in later life. The cumulative effect of their experiences over their lifetime also make gender and poverty disparities larger in later life. Older women are more likely than men to be widowed, and they are more likely to live in poverty, without savings or a pension. Older women live longer, but more of them experience poorer health. Therefore, more women than men need LTC, particularly those over the age of 80 years. A key concern for older men is social isolation and transition from the paid workforce. For both men and women, the risk of social isolation increases as functional abilities decline. The government should support initiatives that increase health promotion, promote active aging, and provide social opportunities (e.g., Elders' Clubs).

The number of older individuals and couples living alone is slowly increasing. A woman looks after her spouse, but when the spouse dies she must live alone with no one to look after her. Even older women who live with their adult children may need to find a caregiver, because the children usually go out to work and are not able to look after their mother. For these reasons, women often need outside care in their later years.[45]

Existing private LTC services are very expensive and unaffordable for middle- and low-income people, who are more likely to experience functional decline and health concerns at earlier ages due to health, nutrition, and income disparities throughout life. Such elders will face difficulties if their pensions or savings are not large enough to pay for care services.

F.   The Way Forward

Key CDS recommendations are summarized as follows:

General aims and suggestions include

- ensuring that the voices of older people and their caregivers are heard and heeded in the development and revision of policies;
- recognizing older people's significant contributions to their families and communities, including their economic contribution through the domestic, childcare, and agricultural work. Older people should have opportunities to train for new roles, including as care providers for other older people who need LTC support;
- building an LTC system on a foundation of home- and community-based care and supports for family members who provide LTC. Institutional care and housing are needed for elders who need complex care and lack informal care support or the means to purchase private care;
- ensuring integration of LTC services through a single point of entry and case management responsibility, drawing together community, local authorities, and health and social systems. Consider building LTC into the primary health care (PHC) system by utilizing PHC facilities and healthy lifestyle centers;
- ensuring quality management of various care services, including those provided by public, private for-profit, and private not-for-profit organizations;
- increasing the availability of a qualified care workforce;
- ensuring an affordable system for older persons, their families, and the government through design choices based on a clear understanding of needs and strong planning;
- ensuring affordable care and stimulating expansion of LTC services throughout the country by allocating sufficient public investment and developing a public financing model for LTC;
- considering how technology can support quality research, and learning from other countries and contexts to develop an LTC system that best suits Sri Lanka;
- using multidisciplinary teams to manage LTC provision. Allied professionals as well as medical professionals should be trained to care for older persons. Introduce and foster a case management system that uses social workers, and integrate the system with the new PHC shared care cluster system; and
- developing a National List of Priority Assistive Products and improving accessibility to appropriate assistive devices and equipment.

---

[45]   W. Holmes. 2017. Gender Implications of Population Ageing: Rights and Roles. *Asia-Pacific Population Journal*. 32 (1). pp. 7–50.

Short-term (0–2 years) priorities include raising awareness and reaching agreement about the direction forward for LTC by

- developing an agreed national definition of LTC, its scope, and the intention of an LTC system in the context of Sri Lanka;
- prioritizing policy dialogue and advocacy for LTC among policymakers, civil society, the private sector, older people and their families, academics, and other stakeholders;
- establishing a high-level coordination mechanism at the level of the President or Prime Minister, and involving the Ministry of Finance to coordinate all stakeholders engaged in LTC for older persons;
- conducting a national needs assessment to fully understand the problems and needs of elders regarding LTC, including issues of migration and a reduced supply of in-home family support;
- developing a national strategy and action plan for LTC to guide the development of the LTC system over the next 15 years. A detailed national strategy and action plan must cover the key components of the system (i.e., policy, governance, human resources, service provision, quality management, and financing), allocate budget for their development, and identify the key agency responsible for delivery; and
- developing a prioritized research agenda for LTC and beginning essential research for LTC with support and engagement from the government and academics.

Medium-term (3–7 years) priorities involve testing service delivery models and trials, testing various systems (e.g., quality management), and conducting research to prepare Sri Lanka for wider implementation of a strong LTC system model in the longer term by

- developing options for a viable financing strategy that can support the expansion of LTC;
- developing and testing individual and family-level support, including training, financial support, and regulation of employers to facilitate continued engagement in the paid workforce by family caregivers;
- piloting and testing LTC delivery and payment models based on successful LTC systems to assess the type of model best suited to Sri Lanka;
- developing better linkage between hospitals, nursing homes, home- and community-based care services, and older people and their families through referrals and transitional care;
- developing and standardizing caregiver levels and standards as well as curriculum standards for universities and other training and certification programs;
- identifying and training appropriate cadres for LTC home visits, and developing a plan to increase availability of trained professionals;
- developing, testing, and adopting standard assessment tools, personal records for adult personal health, and care management structures;
- developing an LTC information system to manage data on number of elders assessed and requiring different types of care, and ensuring that data are available for planning and monitoring purposes;
- developing a plan to promote private LTC provision and regulating services, including small and micro-enterprises, and ensuring processes for registration, accreditation, and monitoring of private LTC providers;
- assessing the feasibility of expanding LTC to the whole country, given likely financing scenarios; and
- strengthening law enforcement and the justice and legal systems to protect older persons from violence; neglect; and physical, financial, emotional, verbal, and sexual abuse.

Long-term (5–10 years) priorities for establishing an LTC system will require enacting what has been decided, developed, and tested, ensuring equity across the country and for all with needs; expanding, where possible, the scope and coverage of LTC services; and building supportive environments such as housing and transport by

- increasing the number of services providers across the country, whether through government, private sector, or nonprofit providers, or a combination of the three;
- adopting a sound and sustainable financial strategy to support the systematic expansion of LTC;
- increasing general revenue taxation to allow the government to allocate adequate public financing for formal LTC provisions for older persons, regardless of whether additional social insurance mechanisms are also adopted; and
- increasing the prevalence of age-friendly environments through universal design in transportation, housing, outdoor spaces and buildings, information and communication technology systems, home modifications, and assistive devices.

Appendix 1
SUMMARY OF DISCUSSIONS AT KEY INFORMANT INTERVIEWS

The Institute for Health Policy team held seven interviews with key informants identified at the stakeholder meeting to gather information on topics related to the country diagnostic study. Table A1 provides information about the informants, their designations and institutions during the interviews.

Table A1: List of Key Informants

Name	Designation and Institution	Interview Date
Mr. S.S. Singappuli	Director, National Secretariat for Elders	20 April 2017
Dr. Ananda Jayalal	Director, Directorate for Youth, Elderly and Disabled Persons, Ministry of Health	21 April 2017
Dr. Shiromi Maduwage	Consultant Community Physician, Directorate for Youth, Elderly and Disabled Persons, Ministry of Health	21 April 2017
Mr. Samantha Liyanawaduge	Executive Director, HelpAge Sri Lanka	26 April 2017
Dr. Vinya Ariyaratne	General Secretary, Lanka Jathika Sarvodaya Shramadana Sangamaya	27 April 2017
Dr. Dilhar Samaraweera	President, Sri Lanka Association of Geriatric Medicine	28 April 2017
Ms. Lorraine Yu	President, Lanka Alzheimer's Foundation	12 May 2017

Source: Author.

Although the interview guides for each informant were tailored to obtain different kinds of information, the main ideas, opinions, and suggestions shared with the team during the interviews are summarized below.

- Before starting the interview, the interviewer read aloud the definition of long-term care (LTC). Because the key informants were officials involved in institutions working on elder issues and health, they were able to grasp this definition fairly well and had a strong contextual knowledge of the policy and regulatory framework, service provision, human resources, and the demand and supply of care for older persons.
- The consensus among the key informants was that the current situation of LTC for elders in Sri Lanka is woefully inadequate. They expressed that there were major gaps in the need for care and the provision of services to cover this need.
- There was a mixed reaction to the question of whether policymakers and government officials understand the need for formal and dedicated LTC in old age; some thought that they do indeed understand this need, while others were not so convinced.

- On the question of whether the public understands the need for formal and dedicated LTC in old age, there was consensus that there was almost no understanding or appreciation of this issue. While some may be sensitized to this issue through personal experience, as a society the issue of needing formal LTC in old age was certainly a problem that the public was unaware of and that needed more attention.
- Informants suggested that currently available ad hoc and informal services should be brought together to enable provision of more formal and dedicated services.
- The major suggestions made by the informants on developing a formal LTC system were to develop and improve human resources, raise awareness among the public on the need for LTC services in old age, raise awareness about the difficulties and challenges faced by older persons, develop and improve LTC facilities, and regulate and monitor eldercare homes.
- Family care supported by the government through the provision of LTC services and financial support was thought by most informants to be the ideal model for formulating an LTC system.
- The informants noted the following points if a formal LTC system is to be established: lack of awareness among public on LTC will lead to social resistance to change, the cultural barrier to institutionalized care, and financial and human resource constraints.

Appendix 2
SUMMARY OF GROUP CONSULTATIONS AND FOCUS GROUP DISCUSSIONS

The Institute for Health Policy team held three group consultations and one focus group discussion to gather information related to the topics of the country diagnostic study. Table A2 describes the groups.

Table A2: List of Consultations and Focus Group Discussions

Level	Group	Discussion Date
Provincial	Office of the Provincial Director of Health Services, Western Province	7 June 2017
District	Office of the Regional Director of Health Services, Colombo	7 June 2017
Divisional	Office of the Medical Officer of Health, Padukka, and social development officers, Padukka	15 May 2017
Divisional	Elders' group, Padukka	15 May 2017

Source: Author.

Group consultations with government officials are summarized below.

- Before starting the interview, the interviewer read aloud the definition of long-term care (LTC). Similar to the key informants, since these officials were from a health and social service background, they were able to understand the meaning of this definition fairly well. They also had a strong understanding of the grassroots-level issues faced by older persons.
- When asked about their official duties toward older persons, only the social development officers said they had any such duties. Other officials, from all three levels of government, said that they did not have any official duties toward older persons, let alone toward LTC for older persons.
- Officers from the divisional-level group consultation expressed that they were aware of some older people who lived without any support from families, despite needing it. Their living conditions were not good, and it is a sad state for such older people.
- While carrying out their duties, they encounter older people who face many problems. The most common problems appear to be loneliness and neglect. The officials think that this is the cause of most mental issues faced by older persons. Even though it is beyond the call of duty, they find that taking a little time to converse with these individuals helps them a lot.
- Elders are more vulnerable to financial fraud and burglary. According to the divisional officers, this is a major social problem faced by older persons.
- At the district level, some services benefit older people, such as active aging workshops, health clinics for older persons, and mental health clinics, but these services are done in an ad hoc manner. They agree that LTC for older persons should provide systematic and specialized programs and services.

- The district-level officers noted that the lack of a continuum of care and the lack of LTC services in hospitals were a major failing and need to be addressed. They suggested setting up a proper referral system and placing a social worker in each hospital to maintain a case management system. They also expressed the need to increase the number of cadres and enhance the capacity of human resources involved in eldercare.
- Provincial-level officers expressed that no one has identified the needs of older people in a systematic manner. They suggested that there should be a needs assessment survey to identify vision and hearing impairments as well as mobility issues.
- Even at the provincial level, there are only ad hoc programs for elders, such as mobile clinics and mental health clinics. They noted the importance of having systematic annual checkups targeting older people. They suggested assigning a separate medical officer to be in charge of eldercare.
- The provincial-level officers suggested introducing a health record book to all elders to monitor their health status, like the system in place to record the health status of infants.
- They emphasized the importance of having good intersectoral coordination once the LTC system is in place.

The focus group discussion held with elders is summarized below.

- Before beginning the interview, the interviewer read out the definition of LTC. The group had some difficulty understanding this definition.
- Participants were asked what health and social problems they face in old age. They responded that they faced difficulties in mobility, vision and hearing impairments, stress from family responsibilities, and financial insecurity.
- The elders said that they were aware of people who are unable to perform basic activities (such as eating, bathing, washing, walking) and look after themselves due to a physical or mental condition. They expressed that these kinds of individuals and their families require financial assistance and assistive devices.
- They said that one major problem faced by elders was loneliness.
- They suggested that community groups can provide mental support to lonely elders.

Appendix 3
EXTRACT FROM THE SRI LANKA STANDARDS 1506:2015

- All eldercare homes must be registered with the National Secretariat for Elders and/or the National or Provincial Department of Social Services, and this certificate of registration must be displayed at the entrance to the eldercare home.
- The home must be surrounded by a border wall or fence and have a gate that can be locked.
- The home and garden areas must be kept clean to avoid the breeding of flies and mosquitoes.
- Manual or electronic alarms must be placed in all toilets, bedrooms, and common areas.
- One-seventh of the surface area of the building must be fitted with doors and windows to allow for adequate light to flow in and for ventilation.
- Window handles must be at a height reachable by someone in a wheelchair and windows must be secured with a safety grill if necessary.
- Handrails must be easy to grip and be strong enough to bear the weight of a person.
- If handrails are fitted to the walls, there should be adequate space between the walls and handrails.
- The handrails must be of a different color than the surrounding area to provide contrast so that they are easily visible.
- Wheelchair ramps must be a minimum of 900 millimeters wide.
- Each resident must have a bedroom area that measures at least 36 square feet. No more than four residents should share a bedroom.
- All residents must be supplied with a bed, mattress, pillows, lockable cupboard, and any other necessary furniture and fittings (mosquito nets, instead of any other mosquito repelling agents, must be supplied if necessary).
- The dining room must have space to accommodate all residents and be equipped with tables and chairs. Each resident must have an area measuring 75 centimeters x 45 centimeters for himself or herself in the dining room.
- Each resident must be supplied with his or her own plate, cup, and cutlery.
- A common/relaxing area to host visitors should be made available and equipped with chairs and tables. This area must be supplied with newspapers, books, a television, a radio, and any other recreational items.
- There must be enough toilets to maintain a ratio of five residents per toilet.
- There must be toilets for the use of those in wheelchairs and other persons with disabilities.
- To avoid the spread of diseases and to clean any stained clothes, such items must be washed at a temperature of 65°C for a minimum of 10 minutes.
- Residents must be provided with nutritious meals, free of contaminants and other harmful products. Any dietary requirements of the resident must be adhered to.
- Each resident must go through a dental and medical screening test at least twice a year.
- Walking sticks or walking aids must be provided to residents as required.

Appendix 4
ADDITIONAL TABLES AND FIGURES

Figure A4.1: Dependency Ratios, Sri Lanka 2015–2115

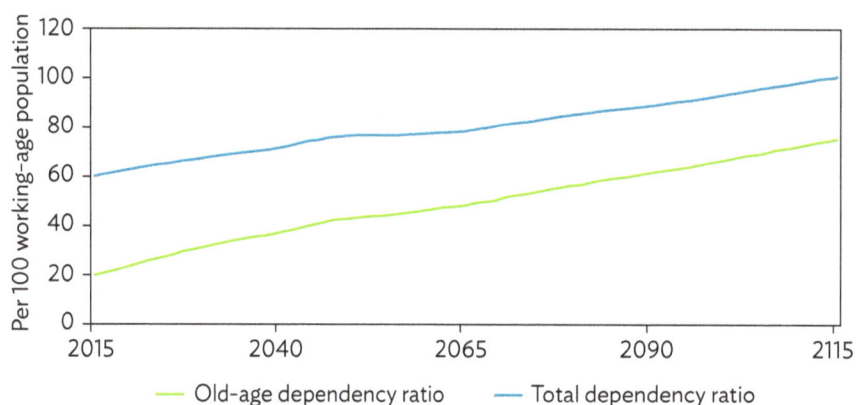

Source: Long-term population projections for Sri Lanka 2015-2115 by A.T.P.L. Abeykoon and I. de Silva. 2016. (unpublished).

Figure A4.2: Medical and Nursing Care Providers for Eldercare Home Residents that Responded to Survey

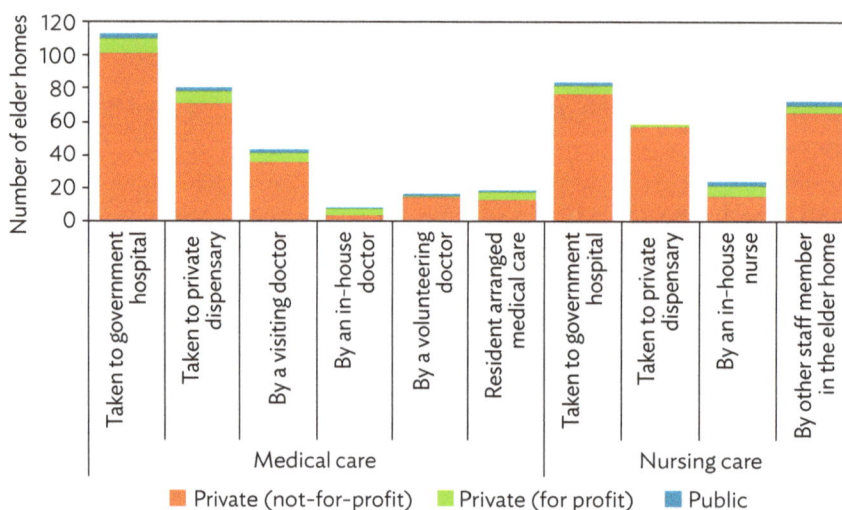

Source: Institute for Health Policy. 2017. Survey of Elder Care Provider Institutions. Colombo.

Table A4.1: Inability to Perform Activities by Living Arrangement, 2006
(%)

Activity	Alone	With Spouse Only	With Spouse and Children	With Children Only	With Spouse and Others	Other Living Arrangements	Total
Activity of Daily Living							
Unable to eat without assistance	2.7	8.8	30.1	50.4	0.9	7.1	100.0
Unable to dress without help	3.4	6.8	26.7	56.2	0.7	6.2	100.0
Unable to go to the toilet without help	3.4	8.2	27.1	54.1	1.9	5.3	100.0
Unable to bathe without help	3.7	6.1	24.1	59.9	1.3	4.8	100.0
Unable to stand up from sitting on a chair without help	4.6	7.0	22.8	56.9	1.9	6.8	100.0
Instrumental Activity of Daily Living							
Unable to prepare meals	3.5	6.0	27.4	55.3	1.9	5.8	100.0
Unable to take medication	3.9	4.2	26.0	59.2	1.0	5.8	100.0
Unable to shop for food/obtain food from usual source	3.2	5.3	22.8	62.2	1.1	5.5	100.0
Unable to manage money/finances	3.4	4.0	23.5	61.3	0.6	7.1	100.0
Unable to sweep the floor or yard	3.4	6.3	25.6	57.8	1.6	5.2	100.0

Note: Those who responded with "have trouble performing" and "unable to perform" were taken as having an inability to perform the task by themselves.

Source: Author's calculations based on World Bank. 2006. Sri Lanka Aging Survey.

Table A4.2: Estimated Number of Residents by Province and Type of Eldercare Home, 2017

Province	Residents (no.)	Residents (%)		
		Public	Private (for profit)	Private (not-for-profit)
Western	3,300	1	11	87
Southern	1,400	9	1	97
North Western	650	...	6	94
Central	400	...	...	100
Sabaragamuwa	450	...	11	89
North Central	300	93	...	7
Northern	250	76	...	23
Uva	200	...	...	100
Eastern	150	...	...	100

... = data not available.

Source: Institute for Health Policy. 2017. Survey of Elder Care Provider Institutions. Colombo.

GLOSSARY

In English, terms such as "the aged," "the elderly," and "old" have connotations of frailty and "otherness." In Sri Lanka, the term "elders" is used commonly, so this report uses "elders," "older people," or "older persons" as terms that recognize the dignity of individuals regardless of age or functional ability. The exception to this is where the word "elderly" is used in titles, programs, and organizations. In the context of long-term care for elders in Sri Lanka, "older persons" and "the elderly" refer to people aged 60 years and older.

The terms below have been adapted from a number of sources. Those which are directly taken from the *World Report on Ageing and Health*, published by the World Health Organization (WHO) in 2015, are referenced as "WHO 2015."

accessibility	Describes the degree to which an environment, service, or product allows access by as many people as possible (WHO 2015).
activities of daily living (ADL)	The basic activities necessary for daily life, such as bathing or showering, dressing, eating, getting in or out of bed or chairs, using the toilet, and getting around inside the home (WHO 2015).
adult day care	Medical or nonmedical care on a less than 24-hour basis, for persons in need of personal services, supervision, protection, or assistance in sustaining daily needs, including eating, bathing, dressing, ambulating, transferring, toileting, and taking medications (California Code Insurance Code, 2018, Section 10232.9.)
aging in place	Supporting older persons to live in their homes and communities safely, comfortably, and independently.
Alzheimer's disease	The most common cause of dementia. It destroys brain cells and nerves disrupting the transmitters that carry messages in the brain, particularly those responsible for storing memories (Alzheimer's Disease International. Alzheimer's disease.) See: dementia

assessment	A systematic process to collect information on care needs of older persons, based on a set of predefined concepts and data categorization to guide care planning. Clinicians or trained professionals typically use assessment to evaluate the physical, cognitive, and functional care needs of older persons and rank their levels of impairment (OECD/European Union. 2013. *A Good Life in Old Age? Monitoring and Improving Quality in Long-term Care.*) See: comprehensive assessment
assisted living	Accommodation for adults who can live independently but require regular help with some daily activities: hospitality services, personal care, home care. Usually available through subsidized or private-pay operators. Alternatives: extra-care housing
assistive technology (or assistive devices)	Any device designed, made, or adapted to help a person perform a particular task; products may be generally available or specially designed for people with specific losses of capacity; assistive health technology is a subset of assistive technologies, the primary purpose of which is to maintain or improve an individual's functioning and well-being (WHO 2015).
care coordination	The provision of care that coordinates various services around an individual. Typically, it involves a "care coordinator" who ensures goals agreed with the individual are achieved through effective delivery of care by appropriate agencies. Care coordination is most appropriate for older persons who are supported by a high number of different agencies, or who have complex needs. See: integrated care
care services	Services provided by others to meet care needs.
care setting	The place where users of care services live, such as in the home and the community, nursing home, assisted-living facilities/sheltered housing or private homes, care at home and in the community.
caregiver	A person who provides care and support to someone else; such support may include • helping with self-care, household tasks, mobility, social participation, and meaningful activities; • offering information, advice, and emotional support, as well as engaging in advocacy, providing support for decision-making and peer support, and helping with advance care planning; • offering respite services; and • engaging in activities to improve the patient's intrinsic capacity. Caregivers may include family members, friends, neighbors, volunteers, care workers, and health professionals (WHO 2015).

case management	Collaborative process of assessment, planning, facilitation, care coordination, evaluation, and advocacy for options and services to meet an individual's and family's comprehensive health needs (Case Management Society of America. *What Is A Case Manager?*) See: integrated care
catastrophic expenditure	A term used to describe high levels of out-of-pocket expenditure on essential services (e.g., health and social care).
community care	Services and support to help people with care needs to live as independently as possible in their communities (Better Health Channel. Carer Services and Support.)
complex care	Complex care requires a higher level of personal assistance often requiring 24-hour supervision, personal nursing care, and/or treatment by skilled nursing staff (Government of British Columbia. Long-Term Care Services.)
comprehensive assessment (CA)	A multidimensional process that incorporates an in-depth assessment of a person's physical, medical, psychological, cultural, and social needs, capabilities and resources, and is inclusive of carers (Victoria State Government. Assessment Process.)
compression of morbidity theory	Conceptualized by James Fries. The theory that increasing longevity can be accompanied by shorter periods of chronic disease and disability. Under this theory, people live longer and healthier lives (J. Fries. 2003. Measuring and Monitoring Success in Compressing Morbidity. *Annals of Internal Medicine.* pp. 139, 455–459.)
dementia	A loss of brain function that affects mental function related to memory impairment, low level of consciousness and executive function. The most common form of dementia is Alzheimer's disease (National Institute on Aging. What Is Dementia? Symptoms, Types, and Diagnosis.)
demographic dividend	Refers to a period—usually 20–30 years—when fertility rates fall due to significant reductions in child and infant mortality rates. The proportion of nonproductive dependents reduces and is often accompanied by an extension in average life expectancy that increases the portion of the population that is in the working-age group (A. A. M. Shohag. 2015. Demographic Dividend: Reality and Possibility for Bangladesh. *The Independent.* 22 August.)
dependency	The need for frequent human help or care beyond that habitually required by a healthy adult. Alternatively, the inability to perform one or more activities of daily living and instrumental activities of daily living without help (Alzheimer's Disease International. 2013. *World Alzheimer Report 2013. Journey of Caring: An Analysis of Long-Term Care for Dementia.*)

Disability may be a cause of dependency, but many disabilities can be managed without frequent human help.

Dependency can be categorized on a scale or in categories with a very small amount of people being considered totally dependent.

dependency ratio   The ratio of dependent people (older persons and children) to working-age people (aged 15–64). May be split into old-age dependency ratios and child dependency ratios (B. Mirkin and M. B. Weinberger. 2001. *The Demography of Population Ageing.*)

disability   Disability is an umbrella term, covering impairments, activity limitations, and participation restrictions. An impairment is a problem in body function or structure; an activity limitation is a difficulty encountered by an individual in executing a task or action; while a participation restriction is a problem experienced by an individual in involvement in life situations (WHO definition).

eligibility   Entitlement of an individual to access the programs or services funded directly or indirectly by the government. Often determined on the basis of income or severity of dependency.

environment   All the factors in the extrinsic world that form the context of an individual's life; these include home, communities, and the broader society; within these environments are a range of factors, including the built environment, people and their relationships, attitudes and values, health and social policies, and systems and services (WHO 2015).

environmental hazards   Hazards associated with one's living environment, in and outside the home. Hazards may be objective (real, observable) e.g., lack of electricity; or subjective (simply based on perception) e.g., anticipation of risk such as high crime rate in the neighborhood.

evidence based   Professional practice that is based on a theoretical body of knowledge, empirically evaluated, and is known to be beneficial and effective for the client.

filial piety   The virtue of respect for one's father, elders, and ancestors. In the care context, it relates to the obligation of children to care for their parents, directly and indirectly (through material means).

formal care   The divide between formal and informal care differs between countries. Generally it is determined based on whether the individuals providing care are paid or unpaid, trained or untrained, and/or organized or unorganized.

Formal care can take place in the home (home help, home care, home nursing), the community (adult day care, respite care), or in residential care (nursing home, residential care home, hospice care).

See: informal care

functional ability	The health-related attributes that enable people to be and to do what they have reason to value; it is made up of the intrinsic capacity of the individual, relevant environmental characteristics, and the interactions between the individual and these characteristics (WHO 2015).
functioning	An umbrella term for body functions, body structures, activities, and participation; it denotes the positive aspects of the interaction between an individual (with a health condition) and that individual's contextual factors (environmental and personal factors) (WHO 2015).
health literacy	The skills and information to allow people to better manage and improve their health.
healthy aging	The development and maintenance of optimal mental, social, and physical well-being and function in older adults. This is most likely to be achieved when communities are safe, promote health and well-being, and use health services and community programs to prevent or minimize disease (New Mexico Department of Health. *Healthy Aging.*)

Alternatives: active aging |
| healthy life expectancy | The average number of years that a person can expect to live in "full health," excluding the years lived in less than full health due to disease and/or injury (WHO definition). |
| home- and community-based care | Services that support older persons continue to live in their own homes and communities (National Institute on Aging. *Aging in Place: Growing Older at Home.*)

See: aging in place |
| home care | Help with personal care (see activities of daily living) and basic household tasks (see instrumental activities of daily living) such as light housekeeping, laundry, basic shopping, meal preparation, household management; and reminders for personal care and medication (Joint Commission Resources and Joint Commission on Accreditation Health. 2012. *Standards for Home Health, Personal Care and Support Services, and Hospice: 2012.* Illinois: Joint Commission Resources. p. 168.)

Alternatives: domiciliary care or home help (usually involves less personal care) |
| hospitality services | Refers to services such as meal services, housekeeping services, laundry services, social and recreational opportunities, and a 24-hour emergency response system (The Community Care and Assisted Living Act of Canada. 2002. Definition.) |
| impairment | A loss or abnormality in body structure or physiological function (including mental functions); in this report, abnormality is used strictly to refer to a significant variation from established statistical norms (that is, deviation from a population mean within measured standard norms) (WHO 2015).

See: disability |

independent living	Housing for seniors that may or may not provide hospitality services. In this living arrangement, seniors lead an independent lifestyle that requires minimal or no extra assistance (J. R. Pratt. 2016. *Long-Term Care: Managing Across the Continuum*. 4th ed. MA: Burlington. p. 180.)
informal care	Care provided by spouses and partners; other members of the household; and other relatives, friends, and neighbors. Informal care is usually provided at home and is typically unpaid and not part of an organized service delivery system (OECD. 2005. *Long-term Care for Older People*.) See: formal care
institutional care	Long-term residential care provided within an institutional setting, usually a nursing home, care home, or, less commonly, a hospital or hospice. Institutional care comprises 24-hour care and accommodation and may include the provision of meals, personal care and supervision, and nursing care (OECD. 2007. *Health at a Glance 2007, OECD Indicators*.)
instrumental activities of daily living (IADL)	Activities that support independence but are not fundamental to survival; including housework, meal preparation, shopping, accounting, medication management, and transportation.
integrated care	A concept bringing together inputs, delivery, management, and organization of services related to diagnosis, treatment, care, rehabilitation, and health promotion. Reflects a concern to improve patient experience and achieve greater efficiency and value from health delivery systems (O. Groene and M. Garcia-Barbero. 2001. Integrated Care: A Position Paper of the WHO European Office for Integrated Health Care Services. *International Journal of Integrated Care*. 1 June.) See: care coordination
international classification of functioning, disability, and health	A classification of health and health-related domains that describe body functions and structures, activities, and participation; the domains are classified from different perspectives: body, individual, and societal; because an individual's functioning and disability occur within a context, this classification includes a list of environmental factors (WHO 2015).
intrinsic capacity	The composite of all the physical and mental capacities that an individual can draw on (WHO 2015).
long-term care	As defined by WHO in the World Report on Ageing and Health (2015): Long-term care is "the activities undertaken by others to ensure that people with or at risk of a significant ongoing loss of intrinsic capacity can maintain a level of functional ability consistent with their basic rights, fundamental freedoms and human dignity."

out-of-pocket expenditure	Payments for goods or services that include (i) direct payments, such as payments for goods or services that are not covered by any form of insurance; (ii) cost sharing, which is a provision of health insurance or third-party payment that requires the individual who is covered to pay part of the cost of the health care received; and (iii) informal payments, such as unofficial payments for goods and services, that should be fully funded from pooled revenue (WHO 2015).
palliative care	An approach that improves the quality of life of patients and their families facing the problem associated with life-threatening illness, through the prevention and relief of suffering by means of early identification and impeccable assessment and treatment of pain and other problems, physical, psychosocial, and spiritual (WHO definition).
pay-as-you-go	A financing model where contributions (through social insurance or specific tax) are collected and then used to pay for current expenditure rather than saved for future expenditure (i.e., not fully funded schemes).
person-centered approach	An approach to care that consciously adopts the perspectives of individuals, families, and communities, and sees them as participants as well as beneficiaries of health care and long-term care systems that respond to their needs and preferences in humane and holistic ways; ensuring that people-centered care is delivered requires that people have the education and support they need to make decisions and participate in their own care; it is organized around the health needs and expectations of people rather than diseases (WHO 2015).
personal care	Assistance that helps an older person to remain independent. May be provided formally or informally and may be related to

(i)   activities of daily living; eating, mobility, dressing, grooming, bathing, or personal hygiene;
(ii)   medication; distribution of medication, administration of medication, or monitoring of medication use;
(iii) maintenance or management of the cash resources or other properties of a resident or person in care; or
(iv)   monitoring of food intake or of adherence to therapeutic diets.

(The Community Care and Assisted Living Act of Canada. 2002. Definition.)

Alternative: personal assistance

private-pay	Services that are paid for completely by elderly care service users.
public–private partnership	A government service or private business venture that is funded and operated through a partnership of government and one or more private sector companies (U. Sawhney. 2014. Chapter 9: Public Private Partnership for Infrastructure Development: A Case of Indian Punjab. In U. Hacioğlu and H. Dinçer. *Globalization and Governance in the International Political Economy*. Panjab University, Chandigarh, India.)

publicly subsidized	Service users with higher incomes pay up to a maximum amount based on comparable private services. Service users who receive income assistance may pay a predetermined set rate (Government of British Columbia. *Publicly Subsidized or Private Pay Services.*)
rehabilitation	A set of measures aimed at individuals who have experienced or are likely to experience disability to assist them in achieving and maintaining optimal functioning when interacting with their environments (WHO 2015).
residential care	Refers to a wide range of housing options aimed at older persons; including nursing and care facilities (other than hospitals) and senior housing. Typically for older persons with care needs who require frequent personal care or close access to support. In some countries, the term residential care is used to cover institutions that essentially provide shelter to people without the economic means or family support to live independently. See: assisted living
resilience	The ability to maintain or improve a level of functional ability in the face of adversity through resistance, recovery, or adaptation (WHO 2015).
self-care (or self-management)	Activities carried out by individuals to promote, maintain, treat, and care for themselves, as well as to engage in making decisions about their health (WHO 2015).
social care	Assistance with the activities of daily living (such as personal care, maintaining the home) (WHO 2015).
social pension	Noncontributory cash income given to older persons by the government. May be universal (cash income given to all older persons, regardless of their socioeconomic status) or means-tested (solely for the poor and are conditional on the level of income). Some countries use alternate terms such as "old age allowance" or "social assistance," reserving the term "pension" for civil servant pensions and contributory schemes.
transitional care	Refers to the coordination and continuity of care during a movement from one care setting to another or to the home.
universal design	Broad-spectrum ideas for producing buildings, products, and environments that are inherently accessible to older persons, and to people with and without disabilities. Principles of universal designs are equitable use, flexibility in use, simple and intuitive, perceptible information, tolerance for error, low physical effort, and size and space for approach and use (National Disability Authority. *What is Universal Design.*) Alternative: inclusive design

REFERENCES

Abeykoon, A.T.P.L., and I. de Silva. 2016. Long-Term Population Projections for Sri Lanka 2015–2115. Colombo, Sri Lanka: Institute for Health Policy. Unpublished.

Abeykoon, A.T.P.L., R. Rannan-Eliya, and R. Wickremasinghe. 2013. *Study on Maternity Protection Insurance in Sri Lanka.* Colombo: Institute for Health Policy.

Alzheimer's Disease International. 2013. *World Alzheimer Report 2013. Journey of Caring: An Analysis of Long-Term Care for Dementia.*

———. *Alzheimer's Disease.* https://www.alz.co.uk/info/alzheimers-disease.

Asian Development Bank (ADB). 2019. *Growing Old Before Becoming Rich: Challenges of an Aging Population in Sri Lanka.* Manila.

———. 2019. *Key Indicators for Asia and the Pacific 2019.* Sri Lanka.

———. Key Indicators Database: Sri Lanka. https://kidb.adb.org/kidb/sdbsCountryView/countryViewResult?selectedCountryId=190&selectedCountryShortName= (accessed 9 April 2020).

Better Health Channel. Carer Services and Support. https://www.betterhealth.vic.gov.au/health/ServicesAndSupport/home-and-community-care-program-for-younger-people.

Burnet Institute et al. 2016. *Actions to Address the Growing Burden of Avoidable Blindness among Elders in Sri Lanka.* https://www.burnet.edu.au/system/asset/file/2160/8._Policy_brief_web.pdf.

California Code, Insurance Code. 2018. Long-Term Care Insurance, Article 3 Section 10232.9. https://law.justia.com/codes/california/2018/code-ins/division-2/part-2/chapter-2.6/article-3/section-10232.9/.

Case Management Society of America. *What Is A Case Manager?* https://www.cmsa.org/who-we-are/what-is-a-case-manager/.

Central Bank of Sri Lanka. Annual Report 2016. https://www.cbsl.gov.lk/en/publications/economic-and-financial-reports/annual-reports/annual-report-2016.

The Community Care and Assisted Living Act of Canada. 2002. Definition. http://www.bclaws.ca/civix/document/id/consol31/consol31/00_02075_01.

Dasanayaka, S. 2006. Innovative Business Opportunities to Serve Aging Population in Sri Lanka. In S. Sahay, R. Stough, and D. Saradana, eds. *Cases in Business Management.* New Delhi: Allied Publishers. pp. 291–333.

de Silva, H.A., S.B. Gunatilake, and A.D. Smith. 2003. Prevalence of Dementia in a Semi-Urban Population in Sri Lanka: Report from a Regional Survey. *International Journal of Psychiatry.* 18, pp. 711–715.

De Silva, N. 2006. *Female Migration: Gender and Restructuration.* Stockholm, Sweden: Stockholm University.

De Silva, T. 2008. *Low Fertility Trends: Causes, Consequences and Policy Options.* Colombo, Sri Lanka: Institute for Health Policy.

Dissanayake, L. 2017. *Making the Connection: Population Dynamics and Development in Sri Lanka.* UNFPA Population Matters Policy. Issue 03.

Fernando, D. N. and R. de A. Seneviratna. 1993. Physical Health and Functional Ability of an Elderly Population in Sri Lanka. *The Ceylon Journal of Medical Science.* 36 (1). pp. 9–16.

Fries, J. 2003. Measuring and Monitoring Success in Compressing Morbidity. *Annals of Internal Medicine.* pp. 139, 455–459.

Fukunaga, R., Y. Abe, Y. Nakagawa, A. Koyama, N. Fujise, and M. Ikeda. 2012. Living Alone Is Associated with Depression among the Elderly in a Rural Community in Japan. *Psychogeriatrics, The Official Journal of the Japanese Psychogeriatrics Society.* 12 (3). pp. 179–185.

Gamburd, M. 2013. Care Work and Property Transfers: Intergenerational Family Obligations in Sri Lanka. In C. Lynch and J. Danely, eds. *Transitions and Transformations: Cultural Perspective on Aging and the Life Course.* Berghahn Books.

Government of British Columbia. Long-Term Care Services. https://www2.gov.bc.ca/gov/content/health/accessing-health-care/home-community-care/care-options-and-cost/long-term-care-services.

———. Publicly Subsidized or Private Pay Services. https://www2.gov.bc.ca/gov/content/health/accessing-health-care/home-community-care/care-options-and-cost/publicly-subsidized-or-private-pay-services.

Government of the Hong Kong Special Administrative Region of the People's Republic of China, Audit Commission. 2014. Provision of Long-Term Care for the Elderly. https://www.aud.gov.hk/pdf_e/e63ch01.pdf.

Government of the Hong Kong Special Administrative Region of the People's Republic of China, Food and Health Bureau. 2017. Statistics. https://www.fhb.gov.hk/statistics/en/dha/dha_summary_report.htm#A.

Government of the Hong Kong Special Administrative Region of the People's Republic of China, Social Welfare Department. 2017. Second Phase of the Pilot Scheme on Community Care Service Voucher for the Elderly (Pilot Scheme) https://www.swd.gov.hk/en/index/site_pubsvc/page_elderly/sub_csselderly/id_psccsv/.

Government of Sri Lanka, Bureau of Foreign Employment. 2017. *Annual Statistical Report of Foreign Employment 2017.*

Government of Sri Lanka, Department of Census and Statistics. Labour Force. http://www.statistics.gov.lk/
        LabourForce/StaticalInformation/AnnualReports.

————. 2006. *Statistics 2006*.

————. 2012. *Census of Population and Housing: Sri Lanka 2012*. http://www.statistics.gov.lk/PopHouSat/CPH2011/
        Pages/Activities/Reports/SriLanka.pdf.

————. 2015. *Sri Lanka Labour Force Survey Annual Report 2015*.

————. 2018. *Household Income and Expenditure Survey 2016*.

Government of Sri Lanka, Medical Statistics Unit. 2014. *Annual Health Bulletin*. Colombo: Ministry of Health,
        Nutrition and Indigenous Medicine.

Government of Sri Lanka, Ministry of Finance. 2016. *Government Budget Speech 2016*. http://oldportal.treasury.gov
        .lk/documents/10181/28027/Budget+Speech+2016/07f592ff-770f-4d71-8c26-b06de595eab0.

Government of Sri Lanka, Ministry of Health. *National Health Strategic Plan 2016–2025*. http://www.health.gov.lk/
        moh_final/english/public/elfinder/files/publications/HMP2016-2025/Health%20%20Admin%20-%20
        %20HRH.pdf.

Government of Sri Lanka, Ministry of Health, Directorate for Youth, Elderly and Disabled Persons, 2016.
        Report on the institutional survey and community survey in selected areas of Sri Lanka on older people's
        healthcare.

Government of Sri Lanka, Ministry of Health, Nutrition and Indigenous Medicine and Organization, Medical
        Statistics Unit. 2015. Annual Health Bulletin. http://www.health.gov.lk/moh_final/english/public/elfinder/
        files/publications/AHB/2017/AHB%202015.pdf.

Government of Sri Lanka, Ministry of Health, Nutrition and Indigenous Medicine and Organization. 2019.
        Sri Lanka Essential Health Package. http://www.health.gov.lk/moh_final/english/public/elfinder/files/
        publications/2019/SLESP-2019.pdf.

Government of Sri Lanka, Vision 2020 secretariat, Ministry of Health; and International Centre for Eye Health
        Department of Clinical Research, Faculty of Infectious and Tropical Diseases, London School of Hygiene
        and Tropical Medicine. *National Survey of Blindness, Visual Impairment, Ocular Morbidity and Disability in
        Sri Lanka: A Report (2014-2015)*. London, United Kingdom. https://www.iapb.org/learn/resources/national
        -survey-of-blindness-and-vi-sri-lanka-2014-15/.

Grone, O., and M. Garcia-Barbero. 2001. Integrated Care: A Position Paper of the WHO European Office for
        Integrated Health Care Services. *International Journal of Integrated Care*. 1 (1 June 2001). https://www
        .researchgate.net/publication/6891513_Integrated_care_a_position_paper_of_the_WHO_European
        _Office_for_Integrated_Health_Care_Services.

Hettige, S.T. 2014. Social Integration, Sustainable Livelihood, and Social Protection of Elders in Sri Lanka. In Human
        Rights Commission of Sri Lanka and HelpAge Sri Lanka, eds. *Growing Old Gracefully*. Sri Lanka: Human Rights
        Commission of Sri Lanka. pp. 57–72.

Holmes, W. 2015. *Healthy and Active Ageing in Sri Lanka: A Register of Relevant Research Publications and Presentations.*

———. 2016. *Long-Term Care of Older Persons in Sri Lanka.* Bangkok: UNESCAP.

———. 2017. Gender Implications of Population Ageing: Rights and Roles. *Asia-Pacific Population Journal.* 32 (1). pp. 7–50.

Holmes, W., and J. Joseph. 2011. Social Participation and Healthy Ageing: A Neglected, Significant Protective Factor for Chronic Non Communicable Conditions. *Globalization and Health.* 7:43.

Institute for Health Policy. 2017. Survey of Elder Care Provider Institutions. Colombo.

International Labour Organization. 2016. *Analysis of the Sri Lankan Social Protection Schemes in the Context of Social Protection Floor Objectives - A Rapid Assessment and Estimating the Costs of a Social Protection Floor in Sri Lanka.* https://www.ilo.org/wcmsp5/groups/public/---asia/---ro-bangkok/---ilo-colombo/documents/publication/wcms_636600.pdf.

Joint Commission Resources and Joint Commission on Accreditation Health. 2012. *Standards for Home Health, Personal Care and Support Services, and Hospice: 2012.* Illinois: Joint Commission Resources. pp. 168.

Kaluthantiri, K.D.M.S. 2014. Ageing and the Changing Role of the Family in Sri Lanka. PhD thesis. University of Adelaide.

Kasturiratne, A., T. Warnakulasuriya, J. Pinidiyapathirage, N. Kato, A. R. Wickremasinghe, and A. Pathmeswaran. 2011. P2-130 Epidemiology of Hypertension in an Urban Sri Lankan Population. *Journal of Epidemiology and Community Health. 2011;* 65 (Suppl. 1): A256.

Katulanda, P., G.R. Constantine, J.G. Mahesh, R. Sheriff, R.D. Seneviratne, S. Wijeratne, M. Wijesuriya, M.I. McCarthy, A.I. Adler, and D.R. Matthews. 2008. Prevalence and Projections of Diabetes and Pre-Diabetes in Adults in Sri Lanka—Sri Lanka Diabetes Cardiovascular Study (SLDCS). *Diabetic Medicine: A Journal of the British Diabetic Association.* 25 (9). pp. 1062–1069.

Katulanda, P., P. Ranasinghe, R. Jayawardena, G.R. Constantine, M.H. Rezvi Sheriff, and D.R. Matthews. 2014. The Prevalence, Predictors and Associations of Hypertension in Sri Lanka: A Cross-Sectional Population Based National Survey. *Clinical and Experimental Hypertension.* 36 (7). pp. 484–491.

Kojima, H. 1995. *Population Aging and Living Arrangements of the Elderly in Japan.* https://www.dijtokyo.org/wp-content/uploads/2016/09/51-74_POPULATION-AGING-AND-LIVING-ARRANGEMENTS-OF-THE-ELDERLY-IN-JAPAN_Mono_26_Conrad_Lu%CC%88tzeler-4.pdf.

Lai, D. W. L. 2012. Effect of Financial Costs on Caregiving Burden of Family Caregivers of Older Adults. https://journals.sagepub.com/doi/pdf/10.1177/2158244012470467.

Lynch, C., and J. Danely, eds. 2013. *Transitions and Transformations: Cultural Perspective on Aging and the Life Course.* Berghahn Books.

Malhotra, R., A. Chan, and T. Østbye. 2010. Prevalence and Correlates of Clinically Significant Depressive Symptoms among Elderly People in Sri Lanka: Findings from a National Survey. *International Psychogeriatrics.* 22 (2). pp. 227–236.

Mirkin, B., and M.B. Weinberger. 2001. *The Demography of Population Ageing.* https://www.un.org/en/development/desa/population/events/pdf/expert/1/weinbergermirkin.pdf.

National Disability Authority. *What Is Universal Design.* http://universaldesign.ie/What-is-Universal-Design/#:~:text=Universal%20Design%20is%20the%20design,%2C%20size%2C%20ability%20or%20disability.&text=If%20an%20environment%20is%20accessible,pleasure%20to%20use%2C%20everyone%20benefits.

National Institute on Aging. *Aging in Place: Growing Older at Home.* https://www.nia.nih.gov/health/aging-place-growing-older-home.

———. *What Is Dementia? Symptoms, Types, and Diagnosis.* https://www.nia.nih.gov/health/what-dementia-symptoms-types-and-diagnosis.

New Mexico Department of Health. *Healthy Aging.* https://www.nmhealth.org/about/phd/phdo/hage/.

Organisation for Economic Co-operation and Development (OECD). 2005. *Long-Term Care for Older People.* https://read.oecd-ilibrary.org/social-issues-migration-health/long-term-care-for-older-people_9789264015852-en#page17.

———. 2007. *Health at a Glance 2007, OECD Indicators.* https://read.oecd-ilibrary.org/social-issues-migration-health/health-at-a-glance-2007_health_glance-2007-en.

Organisation for Economic Co-operation and Development (OECD) and European Union. 2013. *A Good Life in Old Age? Monitoring and Improving Quality in Long-Term Care.*

Organisation for Economic Co-operation and Development (OECD) and World Health Organization (WHO). 2016. *Health at a Glance: Asia/Pacific 2016: Measuring Progress towards Universal Health Coverage.*

Postgraduate Institute of Medicine. 2013. *The Postgraduate Diploma in Elderly Medicine.* https://pgim.cmb.ac.lk/wp-content/uploads/2016/07/ElderlyMedicine2013-2015.pdf.

Pratt, J.R. 2016. *Long-Term Care: Managing Across the Continuum.* 4th ed. MA: Burlington. pp. 180.

Rannan-Eliya, R., and Associates. 2008. Population Ageing and Health Expenditure: Sri Lanka 2001–2101. In *Research Studies Series 2.* Colombo: Institute for Health Policy.

Rannan-Eliya, R., and L. Sikurajapathy. 2009. Sri Lanka: "Good Practice" in Expanding Health Care Coverage. *Research Studies Series.* Colombo: Institute for Health Policy.

Rathnayake, S., and S. Siop. 2015. Quality of Life and Its Determinants Among Older People Living in the Rural Community in Sri Lanka. *Indian Journal of Gerontology.* 29 (2). pp. 131–153.

Samaraweera D., and S. Maduwage. 2016. Meeting the Current and Future Health-Care Needs of Sri Lanka's Ageing Population. *WHO South-East Asia Journal of Public Health.* 5 (2). pp. 96–101.

Sawhney, U. 2014. Chapter 9: Public Private Partnership for Infrastructure Development: A Case of Indian Punjab. In U. Hacioğlu and H. Dinçer. *Globalization and Governance in the International Political Economy.* Panjab University, Chandigarh, India.

Shohag, A.A.M. 2015. Demographic Dividend: Reality and Possibility for Bangladesh. *The Independent.* 22 August.

Siddhisena, K.A.P. 2014. *Ageing Population and Aged Care in Sri Lanka: An Overview.* Australian Demographic and Social Research Institute. 30-05-2014.

Silva, T.K. 2004. *Elderly Population, Family Support and Intergenerational Arrangements.* Ageing Population in Sri Lanka. Colombo, Sri Lanka: Population Association of Sri Lanka and United Nations Population Fund.

Ukwatte, S. 2004. Dominance of Females in Internal Migration in Sri Lanka. *Sri Lanka Journal of Population Studies.* 7 (1).

United Nations. 2019. *World Population Prospects: The 2019 Revision.* New York.

United Nations Educational, Scientific and Cultural Organization (UNESCO) and UNESCO Institute for Statistics (UIS). Data for Sustainable Development Goals. Sri Lanka. http://uis.unesco.org/en/country/lk (accessed 3 April 2020).

Victoria State Government. *Assessment Process.* https://www2.health.vic.gov.au/hospitals-and-health-services/ patient-care/older-people/comm-topics/assessment/assessment-process.

Watt, M. H., B. Perera, T. Østbye, S. Ranabahu, H. Rajapakse, and J. Maselko. 2014. Caregiving Expectations and Challenges among Elders and Their Adult Children in Southern Sri Lanka. *Ageing and Society.* 34 (5). pp. 838–858.

World Bank. 2006. *Sri Lanka: Addressing the Needs of an Aging Population.* Human Development Unit, South Asia Region.

————. 2008. *Sri Lanka: Addressing the Needs of an Aging Population.* Human Development Unit, South Asia Region.

————. World Development Indicators. https://databank.worldbank.org/source/world-development-indicators (accessed 9 April 2020).

World Health Organization (WHO). 2015. *World Report on Ageing and Health.* Geneva.

————. *Age-Friendly World.* Wellawaya, Sri Lanka. https://extranet.who.int/agefriendlyworld/network/wellawaya/ (accessed 8 June 2018).

————. Global Health Expenditure Database. https://apps.who.int/nha/database (accessed 8 April 2020).

www.ingramcontent.com/pod-product-compliance
Lightning Source LLC
Chambersburg PA
CBHW050049220326
41599CB00045B/7344